Editorial Team

Jenny Birkin

Alison Green

Hannah Norman

Design Team

Ken de Silva

Katey Farrell

John Peacock

Tom Sanderson

First published in 1999 by Macmillan Children's Books

This edition produced 1999 for The Book People Ltd,
Hall Wood Avenue, Haydock, St Helens, WA11 9UL.

ISBN 0 333 78059 0

Copyright © 1999 Macmillan Children's Books

1 3 5 7 9 8 6 4 2

A CIP catalogue record for this book is available from the British Library.

Colour reproduction by Speedscan Ltd.

Printed in Italy

OUR WORLD
2000

Children's Thoughts
about the New Millennium

With a foreword by Ronan Keating

Save the Children

TED SMART

Contents

A limo that drives by itself.

Illustration by Rebecca Gordon
Age 9

About This Book

The children whose work is contained in this book are between three and twelve years old as at 30th April 1999, which was the closing date of the *Our World 2000* competition. They come from all over the UK and the Republic of Ireland, and from the broadest possible variety of backgrounds and learning abilities. A full list of their schools is printed at the back of the book.

In a handful of instances, we were unable to ascertain certain children's surnames. In these cases we have printed the name of the child's school next to their entry.

foreword

by Ronan Keating

The book you have just opened is a feast of words and pictures from children throughout the UK and the Republic of Ireland. It's the result of a competition held to celebrate the UK National Year of Reading and the turn of the new millennium.

The competition asked primary school children for their thoughts about what the future would bring. The entries flooded in and the standard was so high that it was very difficult to make the final selections for the book.

Our World 2000 is an accurate reflection of the way young people think and feel at this special moment in human history. The briefest glance through some of the prose, poetry and pictures will leave you in no doubt about our young people's capacity to be creative, wise, humorous and caring.

I can think of no better way to mark the turn of the new

millennium than by focusing on the thoughts and feelings of today's children. *Our World 2000* is a celebration of the imagination of young people, which will also benefit children around the world through the royalties raised for Save the Children. I'm a great fan of Save the Children. They do so much for the children of our world, and I'm delighted to be a part of this special book for children about children.

None of us knows exactly what the next millennium holds in store, but if we continue to encourage children to be the best they can be, and to listen to their fears, hopes and ideas, I don't think we'll go far wrong. We must look after the children for they are our *future* and without them we won't have one.

Illustration by Michael Palmer
Age 9

Illustration by Ffion Knaggs
Age 9

This Moment Matters

Celebrations

Border illustrations by
Lisa Eadie, Age 10
and Alex Farr, Age 8

Illustration by
Fiona Maverley
Age 9

This Moment Matters

11th hour 59th minute 49th second,
Friday, December 31st, 1999.
At this moment nothing matters.

Not whispering wind in the trembling trees,
Not the damp air that engulfs the wave-beaten beach,
Not the fishing boat, bobbing, buoyantly out of reach.
Not the aeroplanes, avidly abandoned.
Not the train services that cautiously cease.
Not the rumblings of motors that finally find peace.
Not death, destruction and newspaper gloom.
Not talk of war and blinkered hate,
Crime, poverty, inequality and matters of state.
Nothing really matters.

Waiting, breathless, young, old, rich and poor.
No sympathetic nods or a cheerful hello,
Not even a joke or a giggle from the children below.
An absence of noise.
A silence held tight.
A mute moment during a memorable night.
They turn away from the darkness
And together make a stand,
Facing the new millennium reaching out
    and holding a hand.
Common in inspiration, hopes and elation,
Sincerely they unite in a joyous celebration.
Nothing really matters.

Until – 10, 9, 8, 7, 6, 5, 4, 3, 2, 1 –
The controlled chant saturates the air,
They meet the new millennium with love, peace and care.
This moment matters.

Ruth Mitchell
Age 11

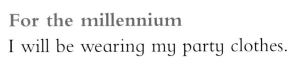

For the millennium
I will be wearing my party clothes.

Writing and Illustration by
Thomas Hayes
Age 4

Rock On For the Millennium!

Illustration by
James Fennell
Age 11

Millennium Groan

Millennium bug, Millennium Dome,
People say the world's going to end, including my home.
Millennium dug, millennium bone,
What's all the fuss about, leave me alone!
Millennium hug, millennium home,
It's 2,000 years since Christ was born.
Millennium mug, millennium moan,
People will party, party, party, or chat on the phone.
Millennium rug, millennium roam.
I'd just like to give a Great Big Groan!

Gregory Davies
Age 10

I hope everybody can be friends

In the year 2000 everyone will cheer
Because it will be a special new year.
I hope everyone will be happy and glad,
I hope nobody will be sad.
I hope everybody can be friends
And all the fighting and wars can end.
Everyone will look after the land and the sea,
Take care of each other, the animals and trees.
People will explore the stars and the moon.
The year 2000 will be here soon.

Lauren Eden
Age 6

Illustration by
Rachael Goulding
Age 9

Illustration by Sarah Attridge
Age 12

I don't think that the millennium will bring too many changes except that there will be a big piece of metal, costing four million pounds, in the middle of O'Connell Street in Dublin. What are we commemorating by this? A new year with a few extra noughts on the end of it, or two thousand years since our Saviour was born? Do you really think a 200-metre-high piece of metal represents the anniversary of Christ's birth? I certainly don't. This is a religious feast, not an excuse to go out and party like wild animals. It is a time when families should come together.

Ronan Flannery
Age 12

*Illustration by
Leonie Whittaker
Age 8*

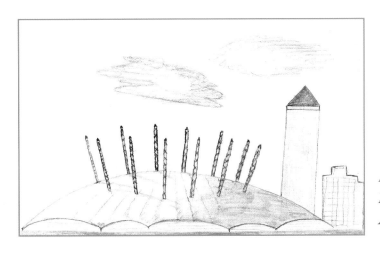

Illustration by
Helen Chatham
Age 11

The minutes have been silently ticking by since AD begin. Back then, they did not realise what would be happening in two thousand years' time.

The first millennium was uneventful. It was the middle of the Dark Ages, so they probably would be too busy fighting wars to do anything about it. So the first millennium was really forgotten.

The second millennium – well, what can I say? They're building a dome in which they will be trying out some very good ideas and some not-so-good ideas, for example, using the rainwater off the roof to work the 672 toilets. What happens if it doesn't rain? What about all those people who need the toilet? They should think twice on these matters.

They were going to make a new *James Bond* film in which he saves the Dome from being destroyed, but they did not make the film when a newspaper wrote: 'Shame the bad guy didn't get away with it. Then he'd be my hero.' I bet half the country would shout good riddance to bad rubbish.

Guy Calder
Age 10

Millennium Sounds

Tick tock tick tock tick tock
DING DONG DING A LING
THE YEAR 2000
W-a-a-a-a-ay
MMMPA!

Tap tap tap tap tap
Z Z Z Z Z Z Z
Waah! Waah!
Drip drip drip drip
MEOW!
'SHUT UP!'

Goal!
HALLELUYA
'Let's have a party'
POP SSHH!

Squelch
'Who's squeezed the cheese!'
'Me'
HA HA HA

DUH!
The coolest sounds
around

*Rebecca Muir
Age 10*

*Illustrations by
Dylan Sheerin
Age 6*

What shall we put in the Dome?

What shall we put in the Dome
To remind us of home
For the new millennium?

A Manchester United shirt,
A yo-yo and a bike.
That is what I would like
To put in the Dome,
For the new millennium.

Christopher Soanes
Age 8

Illustration by
Lewis Walkey
Age 11

I don't think life will change in the Millennium.
One thing is for sure: it will be a party!

Millennium: a party. For me,
Just another day.
People say world peace would be lovely.
No famine.
No suffering.
Everyone living happily.
But this won't come with just another day.

We need time, you see.
Maybe it's the start.
People will help each other.
Care for each other.
But it won't happen. Not overnight.

In my life there's plenty to see,
Places to go,
People to meet.
Changes are happening all the time.
Some are sweet but many are bitter.
I'll do my best to help in any way.
But to me it's just another day.

Illustration by
Lisa Eadie
Age 10

Catherine Puttick
Age 10

The Millennium . . . What a Fuss!

What a fuss they're making,
About one day in our lives.
All the people are buzzing,
Like bees around a hive.

They talk about the Millennium Dome,
It's really such a bore.
I'd rather go to Wembley
And see Michael Owen score.

And then there is the millennium bug,
Causing trouble on the day.
Give it some antibiotics,
Then put it to bed, I say.

What a fuss they are making,
Such a trivial matter, I bet,
When there are wars and famine and murder,
And, of course, the greenhouse effect.

Millions and millions spent on a dome,
That looks a bit like a spot.
You could find more entertainment
Watching flowers in a pot.

What about the year two thousand?
Are we all going to die?
People are making so much fuss,
I find myself asking, 'Why?'

What if there is a World War?
What if the humans all die?
I think, then, the robots will take over the world,
The sun, the moon and the sky.

Amy Donovan
Age 10

Illustration by
Kerry-Anne Irwin, Age 10
and Jade Craggs, Age 9

The Millennium is Coming

Millennium, millennium,
What shall I do?
I'm only small,
There are too many people stepping on me.
There are people here and people there,
There are people buying things over there.
A crowd is coming,
What's going on?
I bet it's 'cause of the Millennium Dome.

Gursimren Lidder
Age 6

Illustration by
Stephen Boyd
Age 8

What will the new millennium bring?

What will the new millennium bring?
An end to world starvation?
Will man share the food with all
Or leave some nations without?
Will there be peace, no child abuse and no illnesses?

Will there be new inventions, more computers,
Clap-hand home security, instant hair growth.
Science pushes ahead.
Will people be able to live on the moon?
Will we discover new worlds?

We must not forget why
The millennium is celebrated.
2,000 years of Christianity.
What does the future hold?
Will man turn away from God
Or remember His humble birth?

Will families stay together
Or will they come apart?
Will children grow happy and contented
And healthy in the heart?
No one knows what the future holds for us
Or what it may bring.
We can only pray
That the new millennium is a symbol of hope for mankind.

Jennifer Low
Age 11

25

MILLENNIUM GNOME!

Illustration by
Alec Smith
Age 9

I think the Millennium Dome is a great idea.
But it is a shame they don't have
A Millennium Gnome to go with it.
If they did have a Millennium Gnome, it would have to be exquisite.
With a lovely bright red hat,
And a nice white T-shirt (not too tight),
Big red boots
And nice red trousers.
That's what I think would be nice for the Millennium Gnome.
Just think, next time it could be pink.

Emily Green
Age 8

Illustration by
Dylan Sheerin
Age 6

This is Exciting!

Hopes and Fears for the New Millennium

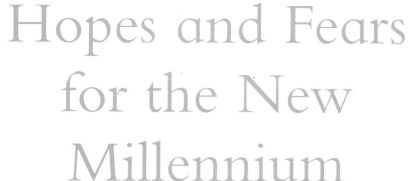

Border illustrations by
Rahul Ibrahim
Age 9

There will be houses on the moon, and Yankee Burger, McDonald's and Burger King will have supermarkets there. People will have green or purple skin, and have ripped clothes.

Schools could be on Earth but you could go on a flying bus to school and see colourful planets with circles round them. The teacher will teach them Logic and History every day, and you could turn into a football player if you were a boy and if you were a girl you could turn into a flying horse.

Rosanna Van Dijk
Age 6

Illustration by
Debbie Smith
Age 9

What will our world be like in a few hundred years?
I think maybe people will still cry tears.
I think that maybe people will still laugh and play.
I hope that our world will not be all coloured grey.

Polly Luce
Age 8

A little girl just like me

Illustration by
Stephanie Male
Age 5

In the future there will be
A little girl just like me.
She will play with the same toys and dolls
But she will go into space for her hols.
She will look back and think it strange
That we had no spaceships, only aeroplanes.
In her house maybe, like in mine,
She will stand and look so fine
In her clothes of silver and black.
Her favourite game is to think back
On what life was like in this time,
The year of 1999.

Jessica Turner
Age 6

I'm looking forward to the next century because, for example, I think there will be plants that will water themselves and grow big and strong so we don't have to water them. There might even be more toy shops around towns. I would love that.

I wish, I wish, that the fighting and bombing would stop and then people could live in their homes again.

If I have children they might want to go on holiday to Disneyland, Paris. It would be great if they had more rides to go on. When my children go to school they might learn languages like German or Greek in a new way, straight into their memory. That would be good.

Danielle Paris
Age 7

Illustration by James Ball
Age 11

Silver suits with space boots

What shall we wear,
I hear you ask, in the year 2000?
Silver suits with space boots,
Sequins, leather trousers,
Hair dyed purple, orange or green,
Make-up quite a sight to be seen,
Houses built in just a day,
Out of mud, straw or hay.
No more school, hip hip hooray!
Or maybe school that lasts all day.
McDonald's grow on every street
Serving meals so good to eat.
Cars no longer run on fuel,
All our air is clean and pure.
What will the next millennium bring?
A better life for us to live in.

*Illustrations by
Stuart Mitchell
Age 9*

*Lauren Jennings
Age 7*

In the year 2000:

- Fashion will be black, white, purple, gold, silver. Because it's Fashion, MAN!
- E.T. will phone home finally.
- We will get invaded by aliens who look like Elvis Presley.

*Sara Saeed
Age 9*

Will we have a trip to the moon for a holiday? Will there be an invention that will warp you to Didsbury or wherever you want? Maybe I could scare my brother by going invisible! Will there be a bridge or a tunnel to America from England? Maybe animals will be able to talk to us! Computers will have more memories. Transport will be different, no pollution! The millennium will be great! The millennium will be exciting! I can't wait for it to come.

Andrew McGowan
Age 7

Illustration by
Laurence Allen
Age 8

I think they will make a car that drives itself. I think that, if I dream, a bubble will come up. There will be a vacuum cleaner that doesn't make a noise at all and a remote control car and it can do back flips in the air. And Skipton swimming pool will be deeper.

Elliott Rhodes
Age 7

In the millennium food will be fast. Robots could do everything. You could have a holiday on the moon. I am blasting with ideas.

I think it would be exciting to have a chute to the downstairs and it could get you ready for school. There would be fast cookers. There would be a robot who does your homework. Cars could have maps in them which tell you where to go. Robot boosters on the car make me go fast.

This is exciting. I wonder what is going to happen. Maybe I will have a job. Or will we live in space or on Mars? I am looking forward to this fun.

Joseph Bevan
Age 7

Illustration by Rhian Thomas
Age 8

This is Exciting!

I am very excited about what clothes
will be like in the millennium
and what food will be like.
Will the food be like a piece of blueberry bun,
all tasting the same?
Will clothes be a piece of sack?
What will cars be like?
Will they be a spaceship or a normal car?
What will holidays be like?
Will we holiday in Mars or just in space?
What will jobs be like?
Will they be in space or in a computer?
What will schools be like?
Will there be the cane for naughty boys
or will they drink a potion?
What will lives be like?
Will you live for ever or just a month?
What will homes be like?
Will there be robots in the house or just a vacuum cleaner?
What will the towns be like?
Will there be lots of rubbish or just a piece?
What will shops be like?
Will they be big or small?
What will scientists discover?
Will they discover that cars can fly or maybe just a pig?
What will I be like in the millennium?
Will I be happy or will I be sad?

Danielle Connelly
Age 7

Illustration by
Rachael Fraser
Age 9

This is Exciting!

Flying cars and different sports,
Walking models and funny shorts,
Birds swimming, fishes flying,
The year 2000, no more sighing.

Robots having breakfast and making your beds,
Bears and wild animals having two heads,
No more trees, no more buzzing from the bees.
The year 2000, all change? Yes please.

No more man-eating plants,
No more wearing of underpants,
What on earth will become of me?
The year 2000, let's wait and see.

Writing and Illustration by
Josh Lane
Age 8

I hope in the new millennium fish can communicate with
man. And that books can read themselves to you. And that
petrol and diesel don't pollute the Earth. And that war is
banned. And that Mrs Bassett never falls off her moped.

Saul Leslie
Age 8

This is Exciting!

Illustration by
Ronan Collins
Age 11

If robots did your chores for you

I wonder if in fifty years
The world we know will still be here.
Will cars all hover overground,
And traffic jams be never found?
If classrooms don't have tutors
Will we be taught by computers?
Will we find a solution
To get rid of all the pollution?
Will we build our houses of bricks
Or will we build them out of sticks?
Will we still speak the same languages?
Will we eat food like sandwiches?
Will we have conquered evil at last
And will murdering be a thing of the past?
If robots did your chores for you
Could they have written this poem, too?

Joe O'Gorman
Age 8

 36

This is Exciting!

Our World 2000

Our World 2000 is going to be
A determined and resolute place for me.
Our World 2000 is going to be
A happy and cheerful place for me.
Our World 2000 is going to be
A hopeful and wishing place for me.
Our World 2000 is going to be
A joyful and delightful place for me.
Our World 2000 is going to be
A peaceful and restful place for me.
Our World 2000 is going to be
A clean and tidy place for me.
Could it be for you, too?

Laura Brocklebank
Age 8

Illustration by Katie Watkins Age 7

This is Exciting!

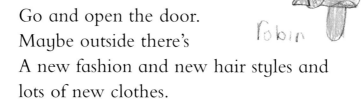

Go and open the door

Go and open the door.
Maybe outside there's
A new fashion and new hair styles and
lots of new clothes.

Go and open the door.
Maybe an alien will take over,
Maybe you'll see a rock hitting the Earth.

Go and open the door.
People might live on the moon.
People might find a new universe.

Go and open the door.
Even if there are only
U.F.O.s
Even if there are only
New tools at the dentist.
Even if there's only
Mammy.

Go and open the door.

Alice Heath
Age 8

Illustrations by
Danielle Benson
Age 5

FLYING MACHINE

I might look like my dad because I have dark hair, but I would not drive a car. I would drive a motorbike with a side car. I might have a computer and when baddies come and the gun is the wrong way round, I could press a button and the gun will be the right way round and I could shoot the baddies.

When I go to bed there might be an eye looking through my window. I might have an alien sliding down the chimney.

Jack Kerrigan
Age 5

Illustration by
Richard Birss
Age 8

A Beautiful Land

In the future we will see
A beautiful land covered with flowers,
The animals are gobbling up sweet grass,
We eat mashed potato,
My clothes are colourful,
My school is in the computer.

Matthew Hodges
Age 6

"Mummy, I don't want to marry an alien."

Illustration by Emma Nixon
Age 8

For fun I think we'd have a pet lion wearing leather boots. I think we would have a machine to make our dinner and a robot to serve us.

I think our houses will have feet and will be able to walk. People's lives will be better because you might have a robot that will go to work for you and do your housework, too.

I think the job you will have is looking after horses and golden unicorns.

I think we will look like models and beautiful princesses and princes.

Debbie Belalouche
Age 9

This is Exciting!

I hear the sound of traffic whizzing noisily by

I hear the sound of traffic whizzing noisily by
And the hum of electricity in the power lines overhead.
Sky satellite dishes now sprout
From most houses on this street.
A kid on roller blades glides by, jeans, fluorescent Nikes,
Mind focused on the rap music from the
Walkman on his belt.
He goes past billboards for deodorant
And overpriced German cars.
I wonder what changes the new millennium will bring.
Pollution, global warming, electric cars?
Shopping on the Internet?
Too many people? Tigers and leopards, even
Elephants extinct?
Millions of gameshows at the push of a button?
A United States of Europe? A peaceful world?
Who knows?
Not long ago people dreamed of cars and planes
And walking on the moon.
If I live to be 100 what magic will I see?

Iain McCaw
Age 11

Illustration by
Albert Suen
Age 9

I hope that my dog won't die. I hope my
mum and dad and Kira and Tara and me don't
die. I don't want the people and me to die.

Alisha Fullylove
Age 7

This is Exciting!

The Past

When the stars were spun into existence upon a single thread,
There was no life. All was silent.
It is the Past.

When the first creatures awoke from their dead slumber,
They were huge and fearsome. Time was full of pity.
It is the Past.

When Adam and Eve ate the forbidden fruit,
The world was in ruin, and considered sinful.
It is in the Past.

When the first car was driven on a country road,
Crowds flocked to see it. They thought it was a miracle.
It is in the Past.

When the present day came, the world wept for nature;
When stars became science,
When dinosaurs became history,
When Adam and Eve became a legend,
When cars became common.

But the future will come,
And the past shall become the future,
Life shall repeat itself.
For it is in the Past.

Illustrations by
Philippa Baines
Age 8

Maeve Simons
Age 11

  42

In 2025 I think girls might all grow their hair so long that it takes up the pavement. We might have multi-coloured cars. Maybe even lions for pets!

Writing and Illustration by
Sophie Nicoll
Age 7

More money from the tax would be given to schools to make bigger and more classrooms. More computers would be in school and they would all link up with the Internet. Teachers would try their best to keep the standards up but I have a funny feeling that the standards will drop.

Our currency could change from pounds and pence to euros. One euro is about 60p and would be very hard to get used to. I think we should not have the euro even though it is the Prime Minister's decision, because I think we have settled in with the pounds very well.

Jennifer Yip
Age 8

We will be overcome by microscopic aliens that control our brains, so we won't do the boring jobs that adults do today. Instead we will lick ice cream out of tubs and eat the sweets that were not sold in shops.

The job most of us will have is teaching adults to grow money on trees and to eat chocolate properly. Then the adults will be made slaves and will buy us as much chocolate as possible. Another job will be to test sweets and chocolate to see if they are poisoned and, if not, to eat them all.

When we go to our friends' house, we will eat chocolate-coated popcorn and white chocolate on milk chocolate. We will drink liquidised fudge and caramel with melted biscuits and chocolate chunks.

Lucy Haines
Age 10

A Money Tree

Illustration by
Cameron Blackwell
Age 6

Either the pay should go up and things should change or you should be allowed to plant a pound coin and it should grow.

Seema Ramanuj
Age 9

The boys have to be slaves to the girls by doing anything for them. They would be paid 1p a day.

Kleary Vasquez
Age 9

 **44**

I think that there will be a robot to work on a farm. I think that the robot will feed the pigs, feed the hens, feed the sheep and feed the cows. The old farmer will put his feet up.

Elizabeth Ireland
Age 8

Illustration by Rachel Morris,
Age 9

Everybody will work to keep their houses. Most of the women would be baby-sitting or cleaning or maybe even running their own business, like owning a shop or having a stall on the market. Men would have jobs like running their own business like a meat market or maybe, but very unlikely, running a shop or a supermarket.

Stephanie Kuhlke
Age 9

This is Exciting!

1990s	2000

Sheep   Sheep

People   People

Glasses   Glasses

Fish   Fish

Cups   Cups

Sweets   Sweets

Fruit   Fruit

Flowers   Flowers

Alphabet   **Alphabet**

Aa Bb Cc Dd Ee Ff Gg Hh
Ii Jj Kk Ll Mm Nn Oo Pp Qq
Rr Ss Tt Uu Vv Ww Xx Yy Zz

Julia Lewicki
Age 10

I Miss My Playstation

The Millennium Bug

*Border illustrations by
Claire Kerridge
Age 8*

Y2K

In the year 999, Jesus sat in his deck chair reading *The Tribune* when a war cloud arose, reading, 'You'll pay.'

'Michael,' Jesus yelled. 'Stand guard. Lucifer shall attack.'

Michael nervously scribbled a note. 'Gone for a quick holiday in the Elysian Fields. Girlfriend Pearly Gates is subbing.'

Jesus was fuming. 'Brainless bimbo!'

Satan was chuffed.

Pearly patrolled, admiring her reflection in the holy water. Then a stranger approached her . . .

'Who art thou?' inquired the beauty.

'I came to see you, beautiful,' crooned the charmer.

'Stop it,' blushed Pearly.

'Except . . .' he began.

'Except what?' asked the floozy.

'Except for the pimple on your nose.'

Horrified, she deserted her post to purchase Clearasil.

Deftly removing his cloak, the chubby imp located the Macrosoft computer (forerunner of the modern Microsoft) on which the world was run. He began fiddling with a knob labelled 'weather', which resulted in eskimos getting sunstroke while camels had frostbite. He jiggled with a knob called 'rotation'. The planet Earth spun out of control. Mothers shrieked as babies emerged with facial hair. CHAOS!! He pressed a button labelled 'HEAVEN TO HELL' and the temperature plunged.

Now, old Nick had been stoking the fire when the coal froze. Satan, on checking his computer virus monitor, was

furious to discover that one of his thoroughbred imps, registered as Y2K, was the problem. So, typing in a few swearwords (password), the imp was sucked along the Internet highway.

This was the birth of the millennium bug. To compensate for Pearly Gates' grief, Jesus promised that one of her descendants would be the hero of the next millennium.

'Take a bow, Bill.'

Emma Roche-Cagney
Age 10

Illustration by
Darryl Hawke
Age 7

The Future

The millennium bug is coming,
It is coming all around.
In bills and banks and traffic lights
It is coming without a sound.

There will be robotic teachers
Who are always going wrong,
Spitting out our homework.
To do it takes so long.

After school we play on skateboards
Which fold up in our bags.
They're cool and fast and furious.
On the back we all have flags.

Then mum and dad hover home.
They're always in a grump.
Dad will hit the laser beam –
The front door opens with a bump.

We'll all come in for dinner.
Mum will tell the microwave
To serve up all our dinners,
And we will try to behave.

Illustration by
Sam Bollon
Age 6

Luke Pankhurst, Charles Harris
and Mark Whatley
Age 9

News of Wales ⓐ25p

MILLENNIUM BUG FOUND BY SCHOOL GIRLS

Writing and Illustrations by Kirsty Ward, Age 9

The Millennium Bug

The school girls, Roxanne Jones, Hannah Simpson, Rachael Hopkins and Kerin Lake (pictured lower right) found the millennium bug whilst taking a walk down their school field.

Roxanne and Hannah say, 'It was quite big, bigger than the usual bug, anyway.'

Kerin says, 'I took my camera in case I saw anything interesting. Well, of course this was interesting, so I took a picture of it.

'I have donated the picture to the press.'

Rachael also told us, 'It was about 6pm when we found it. Roxanne was first to notice it, then she called us over. It was scary at first, then we got used to it.' Kerin says, 'It felt very slimy.'

They also told us it was fierce.

From left: Roxanne, Hannah, Kerin and Rachael

I Miss My Playstation

The Bug Rap

You know the bug,
It's a nasty thug,
It took away all our money.
It made computers crash,
It ate them like mash,
And you heard a big bash,
And a massive crash,
And I miss my playstation.

Eddie McCarthy
Age 8

Illustration by
Rebecca Stearn
Age 10

Millennium Thug

The millennium bug is coming to your home,
Into your computer, we should have known.
He is not a human.
He is not a bug.
He is a computer virus, an evil thug.
He is going out for munchies, munchies on your files.
Put them on disks and run for miles.
Put them in a safe.
Put them in a vault.
Lock it up with a hard iron bolt.
Barricade your windows.
Barricade your door.
Protect your computer.
Never mind the law.

52

Take out all your plugs.
Take out all your leads.
Disassemble your computer.
Take it all apart.
Lock it all up as quick as a dart.
BEWARE, he is coming to your home.

Adam Hepton
Age 9

Illustration by
Dominic Cunniffe
Age 9

It was 8.00am on the 1st of January, year 2000.

As usual, Dad walked downstairs and switched on the computer to read the Internet news. Then he put the kettle on and had some tea. When he got to the computer it read:

```
BBC WEBSITE INTERNATIONAL NEWS DESK

Israel

Reports from the palace say that King Herod is very
troubled by some disturbing news brought to
Jerusalem by three personages dressed in unusual
eastern clothing last night. They brought news of
the birth of a king who would claim the throne of
David one day. Reports are coming in that on the
hills above Bethlehem cosmic lights were seen and
unconfirmed information passed on from local
shepherds is that strange but lovely music was
heard on the hills last night.

                        Reporter: Jonah Elias
                   Reporting from Jerusalem
```

About to scroll down the screen to see the European news, Dad stopped suddenly, his hands frozen over the keyboard. The headlines seemed familiar. But he was sure he hadn't read them yesterday. He read over the news again. Herod . . . Jerusalem . . . eastern visitors . . . baby king . . . Bethlehem . . . shepherds.

His eye caught the date on the top right-hand corner of the screen . . . 01/01/00.

00 – it couldn't be. Could it?

Elisabeth Harris
Age 11

Daddy's Pet

I am eight.
The world is very old.
It's having a sort of birthday,
So I'm told.

It's called a 'milly-ennium'.
I don't know what that is.
Mum says it's a big waste of time,
And Dad's really in a TIZ!

His computer is his pet.
(He likes it more than me!)
He's worried that it will blow up,
'Cos it can't count to three.

I am eight.
I am not very old.
At least, though, I can count
　　to three!
So Dad's pet can be sold.

Katie Hill
Age 8

Illustration by
Sam Broughton
Age 8

Hello, my name is the Bad Millennium Bug and my favourite food is computers and wires. I eat computers and wires because I like to be a pain and get on people's nerves.

Steven Perrio
Age 9

Illustration by
Fern Beedim
Age 6

The millennium bug is a small, ugly, slimy creature.
He comes at midnight to bite the years in your home. He makes a little beeping noise when he needs to communicate. He has a brain as small as an ant but he is the smartest computer. He does something no one likes at all. He bites the years off your computers, telephones and any electrical thing in your home. His feelings are human but the millennium bug cares about no one. Can we stop it? You'll have to wait and see.

Katie McFarland
Age 8

Illustration by
Josh Deady
Age 11

The ruler and the king

I'm the one who's blowing up the world
To be the ruler and the king.

To make computers blow up
And not be able to work again.

I'll be ruler of all computer bugs.
They will bow down to me.
They will honour me and treat me like
A real king.

I will leave man open-mouthed
As his computers drop into history.

Yes, I am the millennium bug.

Claire Kerridge
Age 8

Illustration by
Hussain Mesnani
Age 8

       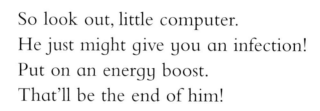  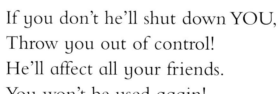  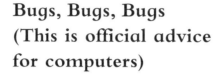

**Bugs, Bugs, Bugs
(This is official advice
for computers)**

The Bug does this:

He steals computer chips.
He snaps CDs in half !
He bites through PC wires.
He blows raspberries at the screen!

He pulls plugs out from sockets.
He'll wipe off saved games!
Look out for this micro-squealer.
He'll give you a real bad virus!

So look out, little computer.
He just might give you an infection!
Put on an energy boost.
That'll be the end of him!

If you don't he'll shut down YOU,
Throw you out of control!
He'll affect all your friends.
You won't be used again!

Writing and Illustrations by Sam McGill
Age 9

Aliens

on

Toast

Food 2000

*Talking Eggs border illustrations by
Lisa, Tidbury Green
Primary School*

When I am grown up I will go to my computer and I will get the shopping list. I will click my name and will shop on my computer. I will say, 'Can I have a can of baked beans?' I click on the baked beans and there in the kitchen are the baked beans.

Ellen Pilcher
Age 5

Illustration by Elanor Geddes
Age 11

There could be a new invention that could be a never-ending piece of chewing gum. It would last for 6,000 years, that's if you're still alive. It lasts so long that it makes your teeth sparkle like a star in the sky.

Luke Watkins
Age 7

There might be strange food like ice cream and chips mixed together or macaroni and mashed peas mixed together. People might even eat worms and snakes.

I hope we do not eat worms or snakes because they would wriggle in your belly. Even if we had to eat beetles or even bugs, I would not eat them.

I wonder if we would eat pens and write with sausages? You might even have to eat paper with chocolate sauce on it.

I hope we don't have to eat any of it. You might even cook your food in a square pan or when you stick your food in the oven it might say a comment, or you might even not have an oven or a pan to cook your food in.

Katharine Coull
Age 8

Illustrations by Lorna Dawson
Age 8

Twenty pence for this big load

My gobstopper is big and round.
If you ever drop it
It will crack the ground.

I got it from the shop
Across the road.
Believe me, it's a heavy load.

Red and blue lines all over it.
It doesn't grow small
When it gets licked.

Twenty pence for this big load.
One day I think
It will EXPLODE!

Writing and Illustration by
Adam Traverse
Age 8

jelly bean
sand
grains

chocolate
sea

The beaches will change. The sea will be made of hot chocolate and the harbour walls will be made of non-melting chocolate ice cream.

But, for the people who don't like chocolate, they can go to the non-chocolate beach in Portsmouth, where sand grains are made of jelly beans and the sea is made of strawberry milkshake. I think this will make more people go to the beach.

Writing and Illustration by
Jessica Berry
Age 8

There will be great big televisions in our houses. If you point at a person on the TV they will cook you what you want, like special cakes. I would like bananas and chicken nuggets in my cake.

Joana Sousa
Age 8

Illustration by
Thomas Clapton
Age 9

There could be a revolution in food and we could start to live on food pills to stop 'wasting' time on food, so we get to work on time.

I personally think food pills, if they are invented, are a bad idea because there are few things I enjoy more than sitting down to a good meal and tucking into it. That's what I think, but other people may take a different view.

Emily Barran
Age 10

I wish the world was made of chocolate. I wish I could eat it until night. I wish everyone was made of chocolate. I wish everything was made of chocolate. I wish the grass was made of chocolate. I love chocolate.

Hannah Caldwell
Age 6

When I grow up I wish I could eat chocolate.

Writing and Illustration by
Jennifer Dowling
Age 6

After tea I would go shopping. Food down town is great, so I got salad, Chewits and a bag of sweets. The sweets are like sour gobstoppers and the salad is like disgusting frog skin.

Ian Dawtry
Age 8

Illustration by
Katharine Coull
Age 8

I will like the millennium because we could have robots in the house. I can get the robot to do anything I like. They could take me into space. I could have a picnic with the robot in space. The food we will have is chicken nuggets with moon sauce.

I'm called Emily, the happy robot

Writing and Illustration by
Catherine Barnes
Age 7

The Breakfast and Dinner and Ingredient Machine

This is a lady cooking machine. If you say a word it does anything you say.

Writing and Illustration by
Marta Martinez
Age 7

Will Our Chippy be Forgotten?

Will our food change greatly
As many years go by?
Will we still be able
To boil, roast or fry?

Will robots be our waiters
And serve up all our meals?
This will give new meaning
To meals on wheels!

Can fish, chips, peas and gravy
Live through all the years?
Will our chippy be forgotten,
Or will it end in tears?

Will McDonald's still be open,
Or will it be replaced
With space-age rocket burgers
And a futuristic taste?

I'll really miss my bacon and egg,
Sausage, beans and toast,
But my knickerbocker glory
Is what I'll miss the most.

Writing and Illustration by
Jenny Cook
Age 9

A Chocolate Fountain

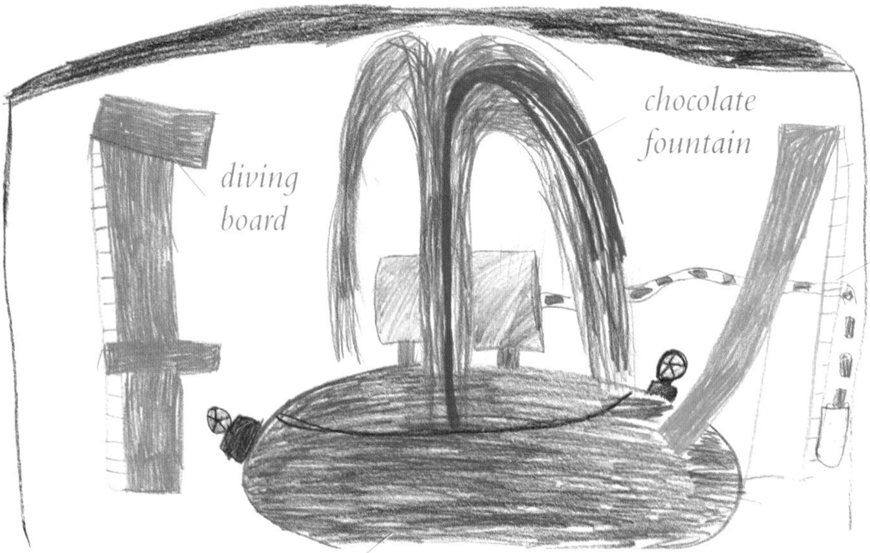
chocolate
fountain
diving
board
chocolate bar
maker
chocolate swimming pool

Illustration by Emma Kingston
Age 7

Food in the future will not be like food today. People will eat tablets and drink water. This will be because there will not be enough food to go around, even at special times like Eid and Christmas.

Everyone will have the same food every day. It will be boring, but they will be healthy.

Mustafa Ayded
Age 9

A talking carrot
Illustration by
Lucy Caslin
Age 5

Aliens on Toast

I'm going to tell what
I think will happen
In 2400.
It will happen!
I know it will!
What? I hear you say.
Aliens!
They will take over us.
We have to do our best to get
OUT OF THEIR HANDS!
'Pinch their suction pods,' said I,
'And go across the ceiling!'
He's nutty. Batty. Nutty or batty!

But as I said that, I spotted a gun
With spots like Mr Blobby's.

I picked up the gun and started
Firing at
The ALIENS!

Once they were all dead
I had aliens on toast,
I had aliens on toast.

Writing and Illustration by
Thomas Swindell
Age 8

  69

Tubey Wubey Fast Food

Mum's coming round for a cook-up
In exactly five seconds.
What to drink? What to cook?
I don't know.

Mum's coming round in exactly four seconds.
The cupboards are bare.
Not even a single sight of food.
Mum's coming round in exactly . . .
Two seconds!

I run to my coat pocket
And reach for a sweet,
And put it on the plate.

Mum walked in!
I handed her the sweet which was
A lovely scrummy
Three-course meal.

So that's what you get, living
In the year 2002!

Serena Birkett
Age 11

**An alien eating
Jupiter**

*Illustration by
Rebecca Davey
Age 7*

The Millennium Cake

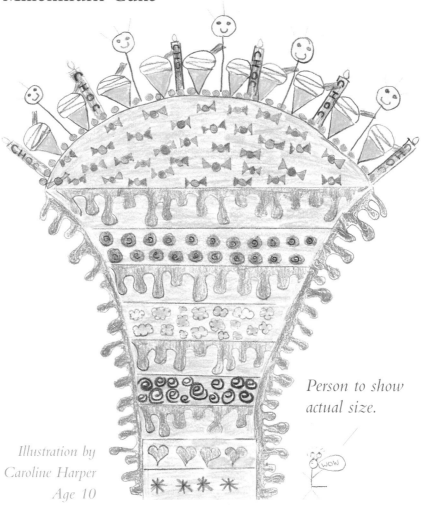

Person to show actual size.

Illustration by Caroline Harper Age 10

I have thought of a new invention. It is a sort of cooker. It has a secret code so nobody can use it. They will have to use the proper cooker. It will change old people's lives so they don't have to walk to the kitchen. The old-age pensioners will be able to operate the code and get food out of it. It is small. It is two metres bigger than an ant.

Kimberley Quayle Age 8

In parts of the world where people starve, you will be able to buy things like banana seeds for a cheap price and you plant them in the ground. Then you water them after you've planted them, just once, and they grow the size of the Taj Mahal.

Rachael Ogg
Age 8

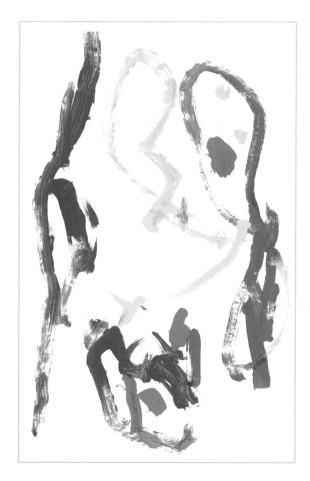

Aaron eating a millennium banana

Illustration by
Aaron O'Connell
Age 6

I think life will be like Star Wars. We will fly about in a spaceship. We will eat alien lobster and drink alien champagne. The aliens would fly to Mars to bring back food for the restaurants.

Shaun Egan
Age 7

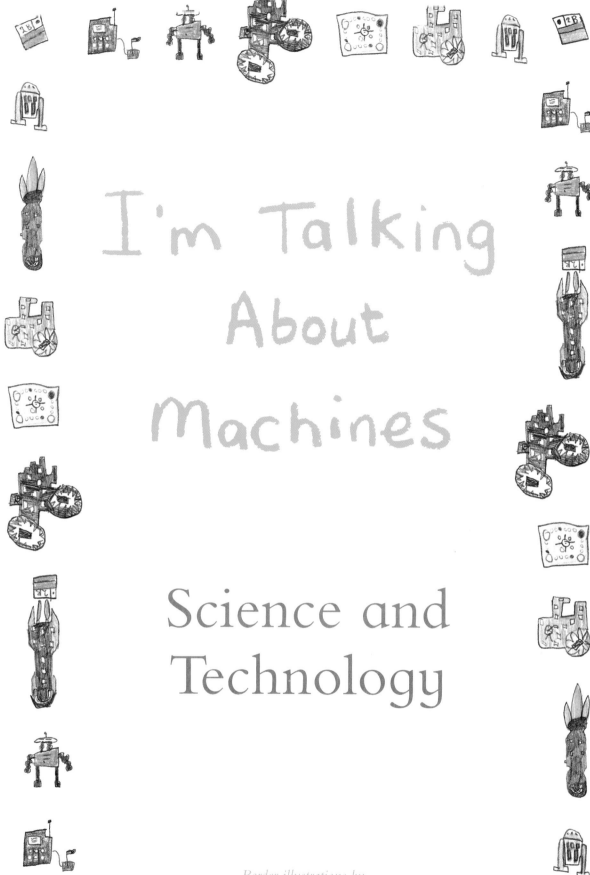

I'm Talking About Machines

Science and Technology

Border illustrations by
Alex Farr
Age 8

 I'm Talking About Machines

INCOMING MESSAGE
01.6781

SEARCHINGSEARCHING***SEARCHING***SEARCHING
DATAFOUNDDATAFOUND***DATAFOUND***DATAFOUND

MESSAGE FROM: BODY FARM SANCTUARY 101.***
CODE:01036/730.***
LOCATION: 3A—132Y.***
IDENTIFICATION: AI.***
OFFICIAL: MIKE MCVEY.***

****

SUBJECT 1: FIRST SUCCESSFUL HUMAN CLONE COMPLETED
YESTERDAY. HEALTHY MALE CLONED IN AN ARTIFICIAL
WOMB WAS TAKEN TO FOSTER PARENTS THIS MORNING
AFTER BEING CHECKED OVER BY AN ON-SITE DOCTOR.***

SUBJECT 2: SURGEON JENNIFER MARKUS PERFORMED AN
OPERATION ON 71-YEAR-OLD ELAINE MEVIS TO SAVE HER
INFECTED FINGER LAST WEEK. JENNIFER LOST THE
BATTLE WITH THE FINGER AND IMPLANTED A GENE IN THE
HAND, AND A NEW FINGER HAS BEGUN TO SPROUT.*****

****

OMOREDATAFOUND***SEARCHING***SEARCHING***NOMORED
ATAFOUND***NOMOREDATAFOUND***SEARCHING***SEARCHI
01.6781
END OF MESSAGE

Richard Stones
Age 11

This plant grows five pound notes every second. And each century it grows £10,000 on each leaf. No other plant can do this.

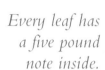
Every leaf has a five pound note inside.

Each coin turns to dust if you do not spend it within a month.

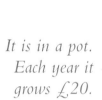
It is in a pot. Each year it grows £20.

Writing and Illustration by Polly Lowers Age 7

People will get better with lots and lots of medicine. Their coughs will get better.

Sharan Dhillon Age 6

I'm talking about machines

I'm talking about machines.
New machines
Old machines
Shiny machines
Dull machines.

I'm talking about machines.
Gold machines
Silver machines
Green machines
Red machines.

I'm talking about machines.
Big machines
Small machines
Rigid machines
Flexible machines.

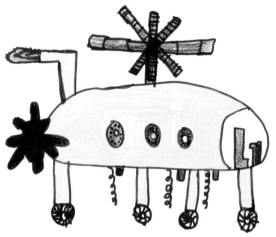

Illustration by
Allan Carnegie
Age 8

Illustration by
Kieran Walker
Age 6

I'm talking about machines.
Blow-up machines
Spiky machines
Thin machines
Fat machines.

Now do you get it?
I'm talking about
MACHINES!!!!!!

Oliver Young
Age 8

 76

Our world is changing by the hour

The millennium has come and past,
The past few years have gone so fast.
Technology took leaps and bounds,
From TVs and computers to electric dog pounds.
GM foods and fusion power,
Our world is changing by the hour.

Flying vehicles, voice-activated phones,
A milkshake to help you lose those stones.
If you need a break desperately soon,
Go on a weekly trip to the moon.
Mini disc hi-fis and microwave power,
Our world is changing by the hour.

Our homes have changed amazingly,
A robot can make you a cup of tea.
E-mail McDonald's for fries and a Coke –
Seriously, it's no joke.
Forget gas and coal, we use solar power.
Our world is changing by the hour.

*Illustration by
Octavia Colton
Age 7*

Space travel now is so advanced,
Get out the shuttle, party and dance.
New solar systems have been found and reached,
The laws of gravity have been breached.
Warp engines have been designed and built,
Our world is changing by the hour.

*Ross Bentley
Age 11*

The Automatic Babysitter

I think this would be a good invention for the next millennium.

The Automatic Babysitter will babysit your children any time you want. Busy parents would mostly use it, but any parent can.

It will bath your children and it will sing to your baby to make it go to sleep. It plays games with your child or children. It cooks tea while you are away. It's like a friend to your children. It also changes nappies.

It is mostly made of metal, but over the arms there is cotton for holding babies. In both hands, under the metal, there is a heat sensor to check the bath or milk. Under the apron there is a tape player to sing songs or tell stories.

Writing and Illustration
by Kirsty Fraser
Age 9

Illustration by
Samantha Perrin
Age 6

Step back one hundred years in time. Imagine what it would have been like: no TV, no radio. It would be like living in a different world. People would have laughed if you said that someone is going to fly to the moon or that someone would design an aeroplane that could fly faster than the speed of sound. You may laugh, but this is what I think will happen in the next hundred years.

Currently we have rockets in space trying to contact aliens. I think one of the space rockets will get a reply from an alien. This will be the beginning of incredible developments in space travel and the beginning of a new era.

We will meet with these other beings. We will share our knowledge with them and learn all that they have to teach us. It will have a great effect on our view of medicine and science. We will discover new substances. We will have to consider all the implications for the human race. It may be the biggest development the world has ever known.

Patrick Henry
Age 9

A Mechanical Future

The pencil we use to write with and draw,
Will be wiped out by computers and more.
The typical things that we lend and borrow
Are here today, but gone tomorrow.

The millennium comes and you'll soon find
That herds of computers follow behind.
Mechanical streets, mechanical books,
Mechanical feelings, mechanical looks.

The millennium bug will come, attack.
One thousand years later, it will come back!
We can stop this problem, there's one simple way.
Let's leave our world as it is today.

Although we don't know exactly what'll appear,
Until we find out we are living in fear.
Natural things like flowers and mud
Will slowly drown in a mechanical flood.

Sophie Aylett
Age 11

I wish there were more people in the future. I wish
I could go to the moon with a rocket. I wish the computer
would give me food. I wish the computer could give me
teddies. I wish the computer could give me presents.

Ria Ginley
Age 6

Brain Swap 2007

- A laser opens up your head.
- A gripper takes a good brain and puts it in your head.
- This grip takes your old brain and puts it in the bad brain chute.
- An injection ensures you don't feel the laser.
- Good brains are kept in a lemonade-type liquid to keep them fresh.

Writing and Illustration by
Michael Rae
Age 11

In general the changes will be that food will taste different and we will use mostly electronic toys for playing and there will be no schools. The most important invention will be flying Big Ben, because if you're late for work, you just press a button and it will come to you and it will tell you the right time. I think it will really change people's lives.

Writing and Illustration by
Isla Thain
Age 8

A toy called the good-and-bad rabbit will be made. It has a tiny switch in its ear and if you are having problems with your spelling, you tell it what word you want and it spells it for you. If the rabbit is switched on the bad side, it will give you the wrong spelling. It just fits in your pocket. In the rabbit's other ear is a speaker, so you can hear what the rabbit is saying.

Writing and Illustration by
Rosie Kinlock Haken
Age 8

January 21, 2314

LION NEWS

The best newspaper around!

Contents

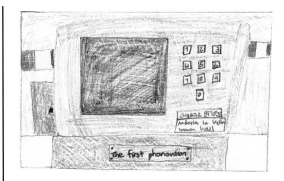

The first phonovision, situated in the Andorra la Vella (capital of Andorra) town hall.

Speak to the world!

CANILLO, Andorra, is a tiny town. The people are still in the 2200 period. But it still has its fair share of fame. It comes in the form of Marco Rhenduit, an inventor.

He has invented the phonovision. It is almost like a 2000-style TV, but is mixed with a phone.

The number is dialled and on the screen the person you are talking to appears.

'I think this is far better than a normal phone,' says Rhenduit. 'It will be almost like going 200 miles for a chat!'

Not only is the phonovision a good invention, but it is environmentally friendly. It is a satellite signal that transports the message, so telephone poles are not needed. The first phonovisions will stay in Andorra, but if it is a hit, there will be the same all over Europe and possibly the world.

Angus Harrison,
Canillo, in Andorra
Age 10

Inventions for the Year 2000:

Hoverboard: A hoverboard will be a skateboard which hovers. No licence required.

Personal Money-Making Machine: A machine which fits into your bags and makes money. Adults' and children's versions available.

Rejuvenating Tablets: Tablets that make you younger. Available for humans, dogs and all furry animals. Be careful not to overdose or it could end in tears.

Electric Flags: Easy to raise when you conquer a new planet. Supplied to all astronauts by NATO.

Computer with Legs: Whenever you want a computer, the computer with legs will come running.

Peace Maker: Zap your friends and enemies and then make peace. Doesn't work on brothers or sisters.

Portable Survival Kit: Ideal for those long weekends on holiday in space. Contains: bed, dried food, water, blanket and useful gadgets. Folds into a 2cm box.

Robot Pet: a pet that you can get to play games with you such as tennis, badminton or football. It only ever bites teachers, parents or any other trouble-causers.

Simon Powell
Age 9

84

Illustration by
Rosey McKinley
Age 10

I am going to write about inventions in the year 2000.

First, I think someone should invent a golf ball with a beeper inside of it. That way, golf players wouldn't be searching day and night for their lucky golf ball. Actually, my mam thought of that one, but nevertheless read on.

Second of all, there should be a mealmaker 2000. All that you'd have to do would be type in the name of the food that would tickle your taste buds and the drink that would quench your thirst and hey presto! Your very own meal! Cool, isn't it? It would be inexpensive, so everyone could have one.

You could invent anything if you put your mind to it, even the world's largest doughnut! I've actually a thousand ideas in my brain, but they floated to the back of my head and I can't think of them any more. Maybe some other day I will, and I'll write another few stories. Until then, goodbye!

Isabelle Kehoe
Age 9

I think they will make a robot with lots of things like:

- an extra long foot in case he's tired and wants to walk faster.
- an extra short foot for walking in small spaces.
- an extra long hand to reach things far away.
- an extra short hand for holding things close.
- a double mind so he doesn't forget anything.
- a homework machine so he can do my homework.
- hair crayons so he can style my hair nicely.
- socks so that he doesn't stub his toes.

Megan Evans
Age 8

I would invent springs for babies when they were just born, and if their mum was getting fed up with carrying them, they could jump with their mum holding their hand.

The springs are not everything. You could have some glasses which can see 50,000 miles and all over China and if you wear them straight and say 'right' they will go right, and if you say 'left' they will go left.

If you do not like that, there's a fridge that has powers and when you put an apple in the fridge it will turn into gold.

Writing and Illustrations by Ellen Wolff
Age 7

The LDD (Life Duration Device)

The LDD can work out the time, date and year you will die. All you have to do is type in your name and date of birth and its high-tech information system will work it out.

I would like to build the LDD because if I knew when I would die, I could make the most of my millennium life. I could also prevent an argument with my friends or family on my last day on Earth.

On the day I die, I would celebrate my life with my family and play my favourite games on the playstation.

Jonathan Lennon
Age 9

I think that the Earth will be destroyed and the human race will evacuate to the moon.

Writing and Illustration by Sam Hussain
Age 9

I have been trying to think of a new invention for the year 2000 and, after many days of serious thought, I have decided what to invent – The Cure-All Tablet.

This tablet would be sold in every chemist shop and supermarket in Ireland. We would no longer have to wait in the doctor's waiting room or visit hospitals for operations. Instead, when we didn't feel well we would take a Cure-All Tablet and get better straight away.

This tablet would be in many flavours so that even children would like it. You could suck it, chew it or swallow it.

Doctors would be very angry because they would lose their jobs. Hospitals would close down and the nurses would also be out of work. Still, I think it's a great idea and would make people very happy.

Linda Durack
Age 9

We will have some Red Medicine to cure cancer. It will help people with cancer live longer and have a better life and no pain. The medicine will taste like candy-floss and will be made out of a new plant called flossy. The flossy plant will grow in Plymouth only and if people in other places would like some they would have to come over to Plymouth and get some.

Writing and Illustration by
Karlie Avery
Age 10

Illustration by
Craig McLaughlin
Age 6

In the next millennium I think we will have a time machine. We'll go back in time to dinosaur times and see all the dinosaurs. Our houses will be villas like the Romans'.

We will go on the Titanic, but this time the Titanic does not sink.

I think monsters like aliens with slime all over them will kill people. The monsters will be as big as skyscrapers. They can pick up skyscrapers and zap them. They have big claws that swipe fast. Our school will be bigger and have ten classes. Our footballs will be made of solid water painted over. The world will be worse because of the monster.

Thomas Griffiths
Age 7

I don't know why we cannot have a new type of person from either Mars or Venus or even the moon. An alien or something like E.T. An animal, perhaps? Even a plant from Mars.

a baby alien

Seeing a close-up meteorite would be OK. I don't mean a meteorite hitting Earth, or it will kill us all.

The dogs, cats, rabbits, hares, chickens, foxes and all the other things in the world will die. I mean, see it by telescope. Zombies could come down to Earth and invade other people's houses and haunt them for years.

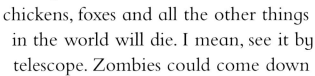

zombie

I've got another thing to tell you about. It is a magic pencil case that does everything you tell it to do. It only works if it is at school. It can open itself and do the following things: close, fly, hit the teacher's head, talk, and howl as loud as a lion.

The pencil case can change the picture on it. I don't mean the old holographic way. I mean properly. The way no one in the world has ever done before.

magic pencil case

I have a got a third thing to tell you about. It is a purple cat. You could sell it for £5,010. It would be as big as my teacher, Miss Armstrong. He or she could meow louder than a lion could roar.

purple cat

It would be great to have a giant creature for a change. Actually, I think it would be nice if it was bigger than a big blue whale.

Writing and Illustration by
Zoe Rothwell
Age 7

Maybe scientists will be able to make androids, then use them as slaves to be sent to places where a real human wouldn't dare go. They could be sent to war to avoid people dying. They could even explore new worlds.

The next thousand years will surely take man permanently into space. Androids could help with this to test the planets for safety. Over time man will rule the whole galaxy.

Writing and Illustration by
Kevin Beggs
Age 11

Initially life in the early part of the twenty-first century will be the same as it is today. However, as the twenty-first century gets older, I think that the following things might happen. I think that people will look different with cosmic contoured hair, ornate and purple eyes and snazzy space-age style clothes.

Scientists will invent weird things like personal spaceships like the Jetsons. There will also be special shoes that will bounce up to the clouds to avoid congestion on the roads. Maybe the traffic problems of today will move from our roads and into the sky and outer space.

There will be no schools, because everybody will have lessons downloaded to them at home by computer, and classes will be attended by video conferencing. Perhaps there might also be a personal home robot that might teach you as well as play with you and tidy up your room for you.

The only sad thing is I will miss actually seeing my friends. I hope the robot plays football well.

Luke Winton
Age 7

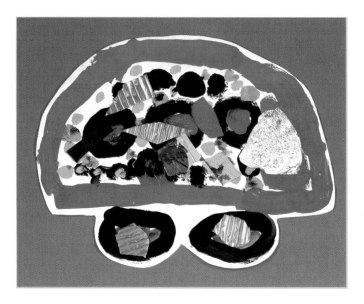

A Jelly Car

Illustration by
Aaron Jones
Age 5

The Computers Are Going Mad

Into the millennium,
Computers, computers,
Controlling the weather.
Switch on the wind,
Blow, blow.
Here come the robots,
Cooking dinner,
Microchips.
Driving cars worked
By CD-Rom.
Brum, brum,
Oh no, help me!
The computers
Are going mad.
Stop them, please!!!

Writing and Illustration by
Christopher Hardwick
Age 7

I am going to invent a time machine. Then I can travel back in time to see the dinosaurs. I hope it is nice. It looks like a hill with legs and it will be bright colours.

Writing and Illustration by
Ben Simpson
Age 5

Inventions for the Millennium

*Here is a
mouse machine.*

Telecom TV is going to be the main invention of the 21st century, in my opinion. Telecom TV will cover 100 percent of the country. It will have a box receiver, which will make sure that the viewer will get a virtual reality picture. With a special intercom for complaints, comments, compliments to programme-makers and a virtual video recorder, the prospects look good.

*Sam Todd
Age 11*

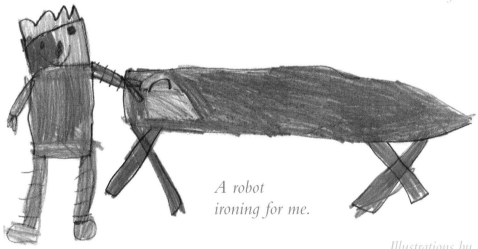

*A robot
ironing for me.*

*Illustrations by
Nicola Rogers
Age 6*

I Love This World

Rocket Powered Fudge

Machines,

Time machines,

I love this world!

A robot tidying up for me.

Illustration by Nicola Rogers Age 6

dog grooming machines.

electronic things.

I Love this World!

Elliot Storey Age 7

If we had escalators on hills, it would be easier for people to get to the top. Elderly people would find it a help to them, because they wouldn't have to walk all the way up. People who find it difficult to walk up hills will love the idea, too.

If we put them on every big hill, then people wouldn't have to go long ways round to avoid the hill. It would be nice if we could have them ready to be launched on New Year's Day. That would be great.

They would be waterproof, so they would work every day, rain or shine. You would press a button and it would go up for one minute, so you would have enough time to get to the top. They would be named escahills.

Laura Clegg
Age 11

This is an electric toothbrush. When you brush your teeth, a bleep sound will go off if you haven't cleaned a tooth.

Writing and Illustrations by
Pamela O'Kane
Age 10

⚠INVENTION⚠

Stealf Camouflage is a substance which makes you invisible. It will be good for spies and OMMs (one-man missions).

Zoe Clark
Age 12

I would like more inventions because the ones we have are getting dull. The most important invention should be Mrs Royal Mail. I think it should be made because nobody will have to deliver letters in future. It will change the life of the men who sort letters. My feeling for the millennium is: please don't change us, change the world. My personal thought is: don't change the world too much.

Writing and Illustration by Nicola Purves Age 9

The envelopes are clipped to her hair.

Her shoes are actually letter organisers.

This picture is of a mail lady delivering some mail into an automatic powerful mail box.

Writing and Illustration by Sophie Richardson Age 6

Dogs Have Five Legs

Millennium Animals

Border illustrations by
Anna Sterrett
Age 9

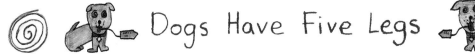

The Piggerhorser

He lives in a cave.
He has scales.
He eats teachers.
He does not like plants.
He has a pig's tail.
He has a smile on his face.
He likes eating pasta.
His favourite hobby is writing.
He is ticklish.
He has legs.
He does tap.
He goes to school.
He can swim.
He is a kind animal.
He has some friends.
He likes reading books.
He does not wear clothes.
His favourite colour is red.
He is always having a nap.
He plays with computers.
He is six years old.
His birthday is in March.
His favourite book is *The Ugly Duckling*.

Writing and Illustration by
Rosie Moody
Age 5

I think it will rain cats and dogs
and when the cats and dogs fall
from the sky the puddles will be in
the shape of a cat or a dog.

Thomas Williamson
Age 7

A Watery Land
In the future we will see
A watery land filled with fish,
Spotty animals munching leaves,
Solid-flavour food growing on trees,
Silky cloth clothes, feeling bumpy,
A pretty school with hard-working children.

Illustrations by
Emily Chamberlain

Rose Malleson
Age 6

What are robot cats like?
What are robot cats like
In the year 2000?
And what are robot cows like?
And what are robot dogs like?

A cow might bark!
And a cat moo!
A dog might meow!
And so might you!

Illustration by
Sami Smith
Age 8

Emma Tyrer
Age 6

In the next thousand years cats will be able to talk English and they will talk about cat food and mice. Dogs will marry lady dogs and on their honeymoon their owners will take them for a walk.

Olivia Banks
Age 7

Illustration by
Sami Smith
Age 8

Dogs Have Five Legs!

Today Tony Blair announced that his dog, Patch, was having puppies at the millennium, and the vet had seen very peculiar dogs inside the mother dog. They all had five legs instead of four.

Everyone was very surprised at the news, but happy for him. Tony Blair is going to call his three puppies Smoke, Princy and Baxter. His children are very excited and can't wait for the puppies to be part of the family.

His new puppies will be part of the Labour Party and will be MPs along with Tony Blair. We also know that Bill Clinton is very furious and jealous as Tony seems to be hogging the TV.

Nearly everyone will be out celebrating on New Year's

Eve, but Tony Blair will be down the vet's with Patch having puppies. That's Patch having the puppies, not Tony.

Everyone is asking: will all dogs have five legs after the millennium? We don't know yet, but we are trying to find out with the best doctors in the world: Mr Taylor, Mr Flimps and Mr Doctor (that's a weird name!).

Damian Kinder
Age 11

I think there will be an invention where puppies
can do everything that people can do. They are very cool. But one thing is different. They don't live up to the same age. They only live up to 60 years old.

The doggy mum is cooking the dinner. The doggy baby is waiting for her dinner. The doggy dad is watching TV and the TV programme is called *Dog Watch*. After that he's going to watch *Doggy News*. They live in doggy world. It is very hot in the daytime, but it is very cold in the night.

They have a silly plant.

Writing and Illustration by
Jessica Lawman
Age 8

Illustration by Fiona Gorman, Age 12

In the garden I think there will be more water features, more flowers and more things for the birds like bird tables, bird baths and bird feeders.

Then again, people may decide to forget about nature and animals, but some kind person may still keep the odd hamster or rabbit.

Abbi Matthews
Age 9

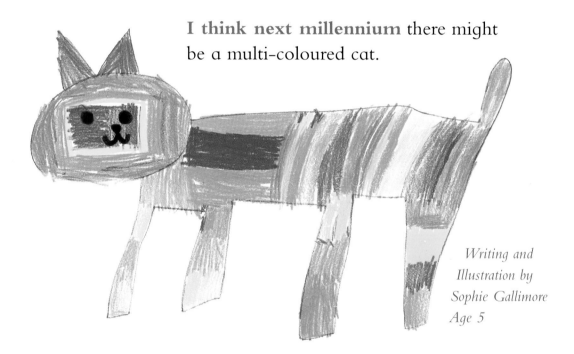

I think next millennium there might be a multi-coloured cat.

Writing and Illustration by Sophie Gallimore Age 5

I really hope all the animals live for ever, especially rabbits, because my rabbit called Tommy died.

I hope everything is nicer in the millennium.

Catherine Barnes
Age 7

All the animals in our days are being hunted, but in the world of the future no one will hunt. All the animals like elephants, tigers, lions and monkeys are being killed for their tusks and skin. People are cutting down trees.

They are in danger. In my world of the future all the killing will stop, no one will be cruel, everyone will be happy.

Alice Dale
Age 6

Illustrations by
Rachel Everett
Age 10

It is 12.00 midnight, and I am standing on the Eiffel Tower in Paris. About two weeks ago, little alien bugs took over the world. They are half a metre tall with green slimy skin, a bit like huge frogs. Their tongues are very long with round suction pads. The frog aliens use their big tongues to stick children to them. Then they dunk them in frogspawn and try to change them into frogs.

Scientists have made a new vaccine which prevents children from turning into frogs overnight. I am now speaking to one of the unfortunate children for whom the vaccine has come too late. Unfortunately I cannot understand him since he has already changed into a frog, so I have got someone to translate. I warn you, he often does the odd burp or croaking noise.

I have just been told that he admitted he prefers school food to flies. Also, the master frog, Slick, has pleaded that the new frogs are to play leapfrog to move around. The quality of people's lives is getting much worse because they are missing out on roast dinners and are having to eat flies.

Emily Sherlock
Age 10

Illustration by Tara Fear
Age 8

One day Robbie Williams went to the Millennium Dome for his coffee and cornflakes. He put his hat and coat on and went for a walk. On his way he met a bunny rabbit and this rabbit could talk. It said to Robbie, 'Hey, Robbie, my leg has been injured. Can you put a plaster on it?' So Robbie put a plaster on it and they all lived happily ever after.

Fabian Leathers-Ashley
Age 8

The Hipop

He is a friendly monster.
He eats everything in the world.
He lives in a dustbin.
He has big feet.
He makes a rrrrrrrr.

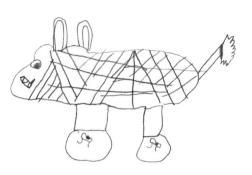

Writing and Illustration by
Luke Hines
Age 5

The Six O'Clock News

(Wednesday)

Welcome to the *Six O'Clock News*.
It has been found that a monster that eats almost anything
including pollution and plastic
has come into the world.
Lots of animals that live
in the sea are dying
because it is so big
and strong and it is
wiping them out.
So, beware! It does
not just swim in
water – it can also
slide around on land.
So when you have got
rubbish make sure you don't leave
it in your house as it may come and mess it up at night.

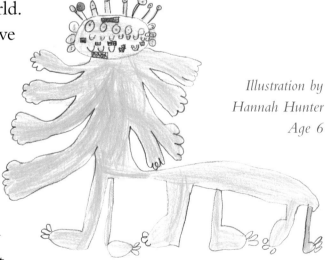

Illustration by
Hannah Hunter
Age 6

(Thursday)
Welcome to the *Six O'Clock News*.
It is now known that the monster has had babies and it is starting to take over the world. It has wrecked about 154 houses. The babies are already eating loads of rubbish and are destroying the inside of houses and knocking down doors and bits of walls.

(One week later)
Hello and welcome to the *Six O'Clock News*.
I'm sure you already know that the monster has been caught and killed. It happened when he wasn't looking. They threw a net over him. It had to be a very big net. He is gigantic. He got free loads of times but then they caught him and he couldn't escape. They killed him.

Everything is back to normal.
That's the end of the *Six O'Clock News*.

Claire Dash
Age 9

In the new millennium I think there will be cats and dogs that can do our homework.

Writing and Illustration by
Anjali Solanki
Age 7

Ponies' Rugs

I think in 2000 ponies' rugs will be very different. They will have fake flowers on and much more twirls and whirls instead of straight lines.

To put them on you just throw the rug in the air and it lands on the pony, then you press a button which is at the top of the rug and all the straps fasten.

Ruth Bond
Age 10

The Horse Hotel

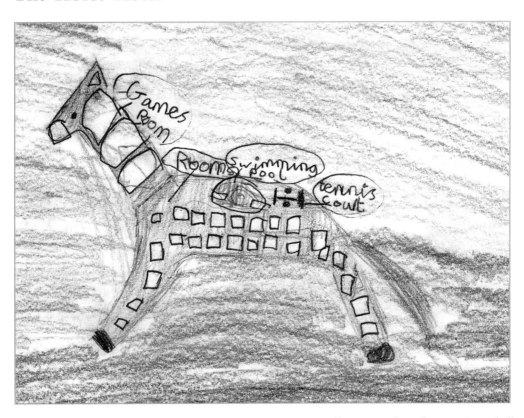

Illustration by Eleanor Campbell
Age 7

Dogs Have Five Legs

In the year 2000 there are loads of things that may happen, so you need to get ready, but I've made up a super idea to keep you warmer than ever for animals. Cats could wear a coat with some very fluffy shoes and dogs could wear hats with a coat and boys could wear hats and shorts with tights.

Cat's Shoes

a dogs coat

Aliens might take over the world and destroy everything, so what are we going to do? Well, I've got an idea: a special potion that will change ants into people so that we will be fine. You'd better start getting ready for the year 2000. You don't need to start rushing. Do what I've said and you'll be already ready.

a dogs hat

Writing and Illustrations by
Kelsii Walker
Age 9

Illustration by
Anna Bonehill
Age 9

When I grow up I wish I could go to the zoo every day because I like animals V-E-R-Y much. I would see camels and meerkats, hippopotamuses and penguins and Jurassic Park animals.

Edward Kenny
Age 6

Illustration by
Helen Fogarty
Age 10

My river has got worse and worse since people started dumping things in it. They started with the odd tin can and now they are throwing truckloads of things into the river. It used to be so peaceful and quiet because we lived far away from the humans, but now it's smelly and disgusting due to people putting chemicals in my water.

Lots of other fish have started dying as the water is so cold, black and murky. The weed and the plants were green and crisp and now they are all black and sludgy and they taste horrid.

The other day I saw a new type of fish which called themselves sludgies (they look like pieces of rotten weed and they eat chemicals). All the rainbow trout have turned black and grey if they haven't died already.

Sludgies have started to take over the river, mainly because they like cold, dirty habitats, which is what our river is like at the moment. I hope that in the new millennium people will start respecting rivers and the creatures in them and we will be able to get rid of the sludgies and have a nice warm, clean river again. Maybe the rainbow trout will come back again. Then the river will be back to how it was.

Rosie Archer
Age 10

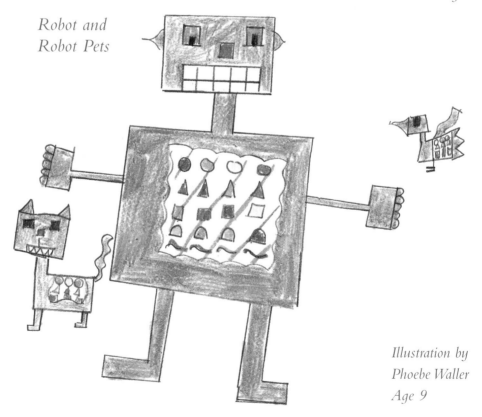

Robot and Robot Pets

Illustration by Phoebe Waller Age 9

I Remember . . .

I am sitting here in my artificial rainforest. It is nothing like the real thing. Only a hologram. There is nothing to do here now. Well, nothing like there used to be. Oh, I do remember how there was lovely countryside and green trees. Now it is only bland grey metal and cyber space rock.

When I was young I was so crazy about animals. Now there are hardly any left. I remember all the animals, like the tiger and the great panda who are now wiped off the face of this dimension and headed under the column 'extinct'. Now they are busy taking lenzymes of normal creatures and mixing them with other animals to create hideous foul monsters.

I will write a book and teach children about the original creatures so we won't forget the animals.

Flora Malein
Age 11

Illustration by
Ryan Scarll
Age 5

I think dogs will talk English and will rule England. People will bark and will have to fetch the ball. I think in the next millennium cats will have to move to Spain and sleep all day.

Grace Fouracre
Age 8

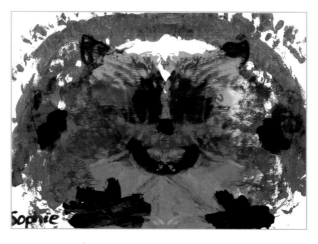

Illustration by Sophie Kerr
Age 3

The cat-napper is a warm basket with bowls for water and food. It has a solid roof and cotton curtains. It is where your cat can have his rest without being disturbed. If he wants to come out you can pull the curtains. Inside there is a little fire with a metal bar cover over it so he doesn't get hurt.

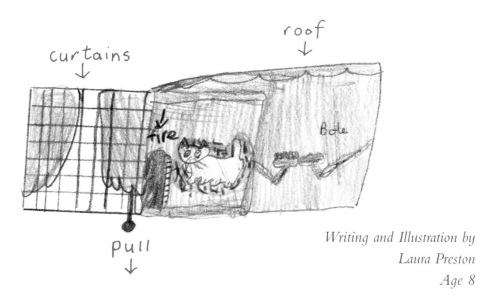

Writing and Illustration by
Laura Preston
Age 8

I'm a surgical vet. At the moment I'm examining a porcupine with bristle brine. Through the newly invented instruments I can converse with him. The large screen in the corner is another of these inventions.

Because of the excellent chemistry, I have no need to put dangerously ill animals down. I don't want to, anyway, and neither would you. Hearing their pleading and begging would soften even the coldest heart.

The new instruments allow me to talk to the animals

Nobody rules now. It's the result of an arrangement that came to be in 2014 on 2nd March. King William announced that no one should rule and that everyone should be good to one another. He was such a favourable king that everyone obeyed, thieves, vandals, the lot!

Writing and Illustration by
Vivien Saunders
Age 10

Remote-Controlled Pet

If you want the pet to walk you press the 'walk' button on the watch and your pet will walk. If you want it to play then you press the 'play' button.

You will be able to choose from a dog, cat, horse, rabbit, hamster or snake. All the pets will look different and like different things.

I think this will help stop animals getting killed on the road.

The pet will have fake fur and will make animal noises. The rabbits and hamsters will wiggle their noses.

The snake will have fake snake skin and will stick his tongue out at you.

Writing and Illustration by
Emma Powell
Age 11

The Turkey Bike

This bike is for turkeys. The box is the controls. D is for drive. R is for reverse and P is for park.

Writing and Illustration by
Sameer Ganatra
Age 8

The animals will take our jobs and perhaps become famous. In this picture I have a cat as a model, a sheep as a producer, a horse as a cameraman, a bird as a soundman, a pig as a photographer, a dog as a director and a cow as a singer.

There is a balloon in this picture and it sends messages wherever the cow wants it to.

There are also magic carpets. That is how we will travel in the year 2000.

Writing and Illustration by
Laura Green
Age 9

When I grow up I will see a dinosaur. It will crush a house. It will carry people off and give them sweets.

Writing and Illustration by
Joe Riding
Age 6

The Cravypavylavyfunnytailtongcordmouthodd-tattoosfunnypatternsfunnyfunnybootshoelacelager-dinosaur

He likes teacher. He likes drinking lager and he likes watching television and he likes watching  Taz on television. He is not shy. He likes shopping, he always buys carrots, potatoes, bananas, apples, sausages and spinach. He can blow fire and he loves people who are called Mrs Roche.

Writing and Illustration by
Ben Currie
Age 5

They don't know which way to face:
the pollution is racing dangerously
towards them, infecting their whole body,
whether with a shell, scales or feathers.
Fumes drift in all directions from the
billions of unnecessary factories. Little do
we think about the suffering animals.
Soon things will change. Legs will start
growing out of all sorts of
places. Animals will become
mutants. Humans will only
think about the fun side of
it. We will make them suffer even
more by dressing them up and
laughing at them.
Once everything has gone
– trees, lakes and animals –
we will notice how selfish we
have been. But it will be
too late. We will have
lost everything.

Writing and Illustration by
Lucy Affleck
Age 11

We Did Not
Not
Listen

The
Environment

Border illustrations by
Alice Dale
Age 6

Illustration by
Rebecca Manguin
Age 9

A Messy Land

In the future we will see
A messy land covered with rubbish,
Dirty animals playing in the junk yard,
Mouldy food floating in the mud,
Dead black flowers on the roads,
A horrible, disgusting school with nasty children.

Rachel Board
Age 5

Our cities and towns will be painted like jungles, and there will be no cars at all. Everybody can wear safari clothes and there will be loads and loads of wild animals. We will look like real safari people. Our jobs will be 'searching for wild animals'.

All our houses will be like the countryside with birds painted on the walls. We will travel to every planet in space. The school will be all covered in darkness, but with a glowing, plastic, pretend moon, and glowing stars. Everybody will be so happy that they will throw a party on the street. Some trees can walk and talk. It will be great. In the year 2000, I mean.

Sophie Kenworthy
Age 9

Illustration by Rebecca, Age 8
Alford Primary School

We Did Not Listen

Illustration by
Christopher Paton
Age 10

The Great Land

In the future we will see
The great land all green and grassy,
Lots of animals with gleaming eyes,
Fantastic food full of colour,
Salad-green clothes, soft and clean,
A fantastic school with entertaining lessons.

Thomas Buchanan-Smith
Age 6

A Beautiful Land

In the future we will see
It is a beautiful land and a colourful land,
Animals eating bananas.
It looks like a moon,
The stars are funny.
Good food in a basket,
Soft and furry clothes
Made of fur,
A rainbow shining in the sky,
A shining sun in the sky,
A scary lion,
A tree wobbling.

Salma Mahmood
Age 6

Illustration by
Lucy Fowler
Age 9

We Did Not Listen

A Millennium Prayer

More people
More computers
More pollution
More cars
More gadgets
More planes
More nuclear, solar and wind power
More war
More selfishness

No petrol
No oil
No coal
No food
No water
No wild animals or trees or birds or insects

  126

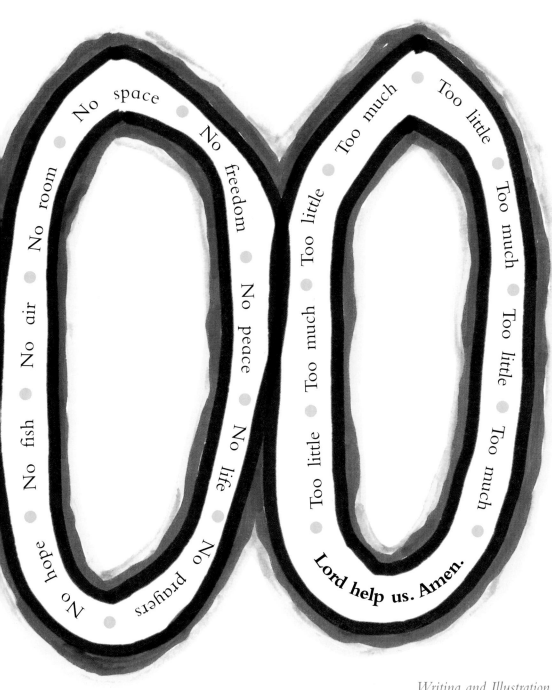

No space • No freedom • No peace • No life • No prayers • No hope • No fish • No air • No room •

Too much • Too little • Too much • Too little • Too much • Lord help us. Amen. • Too little • Too much • Too little • Too much • Too little •

Writing and Illustration by
Giles Littlewood
Age 7

What Will There Be?

In the next millennium
What will there be?
There could be dark green skies
There could be bright yellow seas.

After the year 2000
What might there be?
Cute little fur balls
Or hairy green fleas.

In the next millennium
Who knows what there might be.
Green little buttercups
Or gigantic fluffy bees.

After the year 2000
What will there be?
Fat greyish slugs
Eating every single tree.

In the next millennium
What might there be?
A return of the dinosaurs
Eating meat or leaves.

Illustration by
Olivia Burrows
Age 9

After the year 2000
Who knows what there might be.
Cartoon characters
Out of TV.

In the next millennium
What will there be?
Nature will start changing
Including you and me!

Caroline Sheedy
Age 8

STOP IT!!!

Into the millennium
A damaged world
Crash crash
Trees falling
Bang bang
Dead elephants
Punch punch
Lots of fighting
STOP IT!!!
Plant more seeds
Grow grow
Look after animals
Be kind
To everything.

Charlie Bamford
Age 7

Illustrations by
Emily Chamberlain

Illustration by
Ryan Mace
Age 9

Far in the future in the year 2052, we lived in an underground city, and if we ever dared venture to our old towns we would wear oxygen masks. So here is the story of how it came to be:

We were warned not to cut down trees.
We were warned not to kill animals.
We were warned not to put chemicals in the air.
BUT WE DID NOT LISTEN.

We were warned not to pollute the sea.
We were warned not to disrespect the Earth.
BUT WE STILL DID NOT LISTEN.

130

It makes me so sad that I can only look at the sea and not swim in it. I will never hear the birds sing and the wind blow through the trees. My only experience of these things is on virtual reality screens.

But MAYBE WE DID LISTEN and this is all a dream. Because as I look outside, the birds are singing, the trees are swaying in the wind and happy children are swimming in the sea.

Laura Titterington
Age 8

Illustration by
Kara Stentiford
Age 9

We Did Not Listen

The year 2000 will have less pollution and no wars.
Everyone will care about the environment and peace will be
everybody's greatest wish. Our most important aim in life will
be to care for the countryside and to save our planet.

Also there will be no police because there will be no crimes.
Everyone will have their own solar-powered car and a private
teleporter. If you miss two hours of work, the computer and the
TV will not go on for you.

There will be no money in the year 2000, so everyone will
be the same. There will be places where you will be able to see
wildlife and no animals will be endangered.

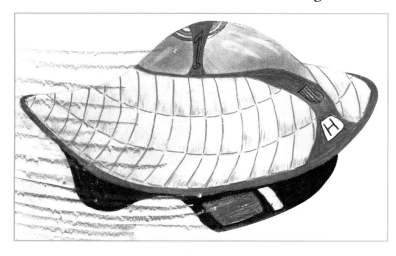

Illustration by
Kevin Else
Age 10

No animals will be kept in cramped cages. Everyone will
be a vegetarian and we will each have our own allotment
and grow all our own organic food. We will all have our own
sheep and from the wool make our own clothes.

Anyone can worship in any way that they like and we
will all respect each other's beliefs. Our laws for living will be
based on Rights, Responsibilities and Respect.

Harry Perston
Age 9

My sisters and I went into the future and we saw fewer cars because fuel had been banned. We also saw no wars, because they thought it was not nice. Also, it was a lot hotter, so there were strawberries all year round. All the buildings were multi-coloured, including the houses. Later we went home and told Mum, but she didn't believe us.

Writing and Illustration by
Geraldine Sherwin
Age 7

I was irate with the nation

Gun muzzles left in the fields.
Irresponsible children dropped litter.
Lonesome trees killed by pollution.
The livid Earth bruised by mankind.
Epidemic diseases killed nature's creations.
The beautiful forests and fields, neglected and tired.
Noisy cars, derelict buildings, cities past.
I was irate with the nation.
The hoary, unnurtured planet was giving up rapidly.

That was the past.

I hope the world changes in the millennium.

Poppy Anderson
Age 11

Illustration by
Jolene Duffy
Age 6

Who knows?

Who knows what the millennium will bring,
Solar-powered cars with automatic wings.
Our houses will grow bigger,
Invading all the land,
The deserts will keep growing,
Turning grass into sand.
Teachers will be history,
They will disappear quite soon,
For computers are taking over –
You'll be taught in your own front room.
An ice age may be coming,
A meteor may fall.
But not to worry, my ticket's booked.
We'll be on the moon after all.

Christopher Gracie
Age 11

We will have to wear a wide-brimmed hat to protect us from the sun. There will be fewer jobs because computers will be doing most of the work. Our houses will have a lot more insulation as energy will not be so cheap. I think we will walk and cycle more, and space travel will be too expensive.

Children in rural areas might be taught at home by computer link-up. Our cities and towns will hopefully be cleaner and safer places to be in, if they are pedestrianised.

As for our countryside, if they don't stop building new houses there will not be any fields left. Within the next ten years I think that everybody will own their own computer and do most of their shopping from home. With all the computer games getting better all the time, we will probably all be addicted to them.

In the millennium, I would hope our lives would be better, but I'm sure people will still talk a lot about the good old days.

Stuart Andrew
Age 9

Illustration by
Dylan Sheerin
Age 6

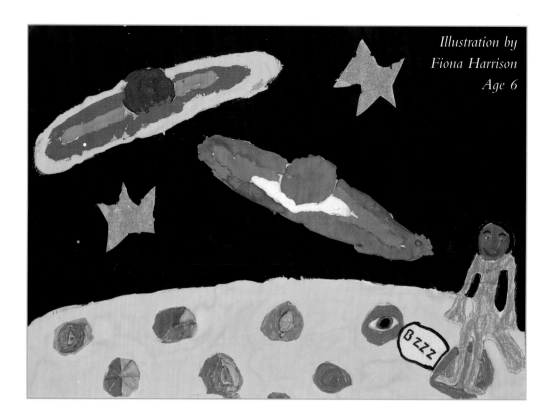

Illustration by
Fiona Harrison
Age 6

It is now the year 2099. The effects of global warming have caused the polar ice caps to melt and cover all low ground, including most of Africa, Asia, Eastern Europe and some parts of North America, and destroying famous buildings and statues.

Luckily, the Inter-Planetary Council launched a very efficient rescue, evacuating vulnerable towns, cities and villages and accommodating them in emergency shelters on high ground.

The world leaders know they can't live with ten billion people stuck on mountains, hills and tall buildings, so they start an emergency operation to drain all the water. They build large tanks which carry approximately 90 gallons of water a

second and put one in Europe, pumping water directly to the moon. The Inter-Planetary Council decide this could actually be a good thing and spend six years building an oxygen forcefield around the moon and a further two years building water-purifying tanks and dome-shaped houses.

In the year 2107, when it is declared safe to live on the moon, at least three billion people go and live there, while the other seven billion live in an almost pollution-free world as no one has used a car for eight years.

Sean Maher
Age 10

Illustration by
Lisa Davies
Age 7

There is a mass of pollution everywhere. People have to wear masks to help them breathe. The traffic is at a standstill. Cities are snarled up. Road rage is rife. Car horns scream constantly.

People are dying of dehydration and asthma because it is so hot. The countryside is just dead grass and plants. The streams around them have just dried up. Could the world be dying?

Illustration by Nathan Markham Age 7

The icebergs are like little ice cubes in a big round bowl. The world would have been flooded but the sun has dried up half the sea. People are fighting for food and water.

Some people are paying millions to go into space to get away from the havoc. People are paying thousands to get a couple of cups of pure water.

Does anyone have a solution to this dirty pollution? Surely someone has. A pollution-sucking machine! City after city, town after town, village after village is saved. Slowly but surely the world will be the place we dream about. The Third World is restored. People have homes and enough food to eat. People have learnt to live fairly and justly without being greedy. Sharing the Earth's resources. Caring for one another.

Jason Metcalfe
Age 10

The Last Rabbit in the World

In the next millennium there will not be a tree in sight;
The country will be a ruin
Like an old ruined castle upon an oily beach.
Already spoilt.
The world is a polluted place
And there will be one patch of grass
And on that patch of grass
There will be the last rabbit in the world.
Everyone will come from near and far to see it.
They'd say, 'There used to be lots of them,
But now only one.
And then none.'
The pollution is growing,
Global warming is increasing rapidly.
It's getting out of hand.
Cars, lorries and factories
Are wearing out our environment
And killing some animals,
Making others rare.
Who is at the end of most food chains?

Adam Wheeler
Age 10

Illustration by
Teresa Lee
Age 9

On November 25th, there was an announcement by a famous professor. He said the sun was racing around the galaxy one billion times per hour. A week later another announcement was made. The sun was aiming for Earth and 1,000 spaceships were being made, so big they could fit 3,000 people each.

The days got hotter and hotter until it was like summer. People roasted. Lots of people died from heat. Some people were having a good time. No shops were open, so people were stealing goods and blowing the premises up.

The first spaceship had important people in it like royalty and presidents. We all got in quite a state. People were running

around the streets in panic. You had to get a special card to be on the spaceship. We got one. We were very sad because our grandparents had to stay behind. All the people over fifty had to stay.

When we got to the launching area the streets were packed with people. We had to wait two days to get in. We were on the three-hundredth spaceship. It was a horrible little room with bunk beds. We unpacked our clothes. I fell asleep after a long time.

When I woke up I did not know where I was, but then I remembered. I found out that only four hundred spaceships had lifted off. I looked out of the tiny window we had and saw the Earth blow up.

Aoife Naughton
Age 11

I have made an invention of a tree car. It would be good because it would be kind to the planet. It will run on water.

Writing and Illustration by
Thomas O'Callaghan
Age 10

Illustration by
Sally Morton
Age 12

As we go into the new millennium, new forms of fuel will be discovered to replace fossil fuels. This will enable us to travel much greater distances quickly and easily and result in far less damage to our environment. By the middle of the millennium we may have invented the friction-free flying car. By the end, travelling in space like we do with an aeroplane may be the craze.

Renewable forms of energy will also allow us to heat and light our homes much more efficiently. This means we can build homes in areas that at present cannot be inhabited, for example Alaska or Northern Siberia. As we go further into the millennium people will develop the technology to live under the sea.

Schools of the future will be very different. Specialist teachers would be based in regional centres and students will log on to their lessons via video conferencing and the Internet.

This will be more efficient and, again, people do not have to live in our typical overcrowded, congested cities. All students can go to a local school and access their lessons. No longer will we need to travel great distances to go to 'good' schools. This will greatly ease congestion and pollution on the roads.

So cities as we know them today will become less and less attractive as people will prefer to live in the mountains, under the sea and in the countryside.

Jamie Sawyer
Age 11

A volcano will come out of the sea and when you are on holiday you have to wear a special suit or you will be scalded.

Lewis Garforth
Age 5

Illustration by
Hadyn Sacker
Age 6

Humans on the Moon

The year is 2841 AD. Before Professor Schleikchzenhahben-leickhen discovered a way to produce an oxygen field around the moon, so that it could be transformed into a mini-Earth, the Earth's population had been rapidly increasing. On the 1st May, 2837 AD, the population of the world was estimated at 291,000,000,000.

However, the President of the World, John Kennedy XXIII, called all the world leaders to the White House and, in front of over 40,000,000,000 TV viewers, announced that the plans would go ahead. So NASA satellites beamed out an oxygen field. Over

144

a couple of weeks it settled and architects and builders moved in.

First, water was pumped into giant trenches that the builders had dug. They became rivers. Then we planted mutant plants, which grow to full size in under 10 seconds. Then we started to build houses, offices, shops and other buildings.

Soon the moon was fully cultivated. Millions started to move on, as offers of free housing, millions of jobs and lower prices tempted them from the Earth's poverty-stricken slums. Gradually, the moon's population rose to over five billion and Professor Schleikchzenhahbenleickhen was hailed as the saviour of the Earth's people.

Richard Partington
Age 11

Illustration by
Emmeline Pinion
Age 5

I think the world will turn more slowly and that rockets will have patterns on the outside of them.

Austin Milner-Cottrell
Age 5

Illustration by Laura Conry
Age 6

The Countryside

Will the millennium bring still
The beautiful bushy trees,
Flowers glittering in the sun,
Animals grazing,
Chewing away at the juicy grass?

Will the millennium bring
Dirty, dusty fields
With thorns growing,
No flowers,
Just dead weeds?

  146

Will people visit the merry, friendly animals,
Dancing and leaping with joy,
Or will they turn nasty
With their eyes bursting with fire?

Will you pick some red juicy apples off the trees?
Or brown, soft, sour, rotten ones
From the dead branches?

I wonder what the millennium
Will bring to our countryside?

Jessica Parker
Age 8

I drew a weather machine for the next millennium.
You can touch any button for the weather
you want, then touch the enter button. Then
there is a 'strength' button you touch. You touch
any number you want:

1 VERY WEAK
2 QUITE WEAK
3 NOT A LOT OF WEAKNESS
4 A LITTLE BIT STRONG
5 QUITE STRONG
6 VERY STRONG

You press any number, then press
'go out' and the weather you have
chosen will come out of the pipe.

Writing and Illustration
by Kim Munnery
Age 8

Millennium Speech

My name is Alexander Maguire. I work as a research officer on weather.

A giant asteroid will hit the sun in round about five years' time, causing the sun to split in two. The two parts will drift close around the Earth. It will not be close enough to burn up the Earth, but close enough to be an everlasting summer.

Sounds good? I don't think so. It will be so hot we won't be able to live on dry land. We will only be able to live out in the open for two hours at the very most.

There is only one option. We must build domes underwater to live in. Thousands and thousands of them. We have to start getting food and water now! It's the only option.

So, are you in, or are you out?

Luke Barnes
Age 11

Illustration by
Jeong-Min Park
Age 9

Our
Teacher
is a
Robot

School

Border illustrations by
Thomas Dent
Age 9

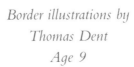

When you spell a spelling wrong, a beeper beeps because you have got a word wrong. There is a screen on the pen and you look at the screen and then it shows you how to spell it. The beeper can make different noises. When you get it right it makes a different noise. If it's an easy word, it doesn't beep because it knows that you can spell it, and the beeper rubs out, but it can't break.

Writing and Illustration by
Jenni Petty
Age 6

This is my school. I changed it to a mobile school instead of a mobile home.

Writing and Illustration by
Leanne Macfarlane
Age 10

I drew a flying school, and it can go left and right and up and down. The children all love to go there.

Writing and Illustration by
Michael Kennedy
Age 5

I think we will go to school and play with the toys every day at school, and when there is fruit and drink, we will throw them all over the place.

I think we will dress up like it was the olden days and I think we will play hide-and-seek.

Lee Morrow
Age 5

Illustration by Scott
Mid Calder Primary School

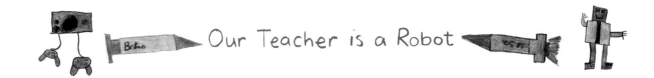

I would like to make the school fly when we're working.

Writing and Illustration by
Georgie Hayhurst
Age 7

There will need to be more jobs because there will be more people in the world. I want to be a teacher when I am older because it looks good. I asked some of my friends. Sam said he wants to be a policeman. Sarah wants to be a vet and so does Emma and Hazel wants to be an artist. Hannah wants to be a teacher as well as me.

Natalie Reid
Age 8

One day I woke up, with the sun streaming through my window, when I heard someone saying, 'Wake up, Jamie, it's breakfast time.' Then I remembered it was only my talking alarm clock. It was as small as a gnome.

I went downstairs, and suddenly a hand shot out with my

breakfast. I ate it all very quickly. I went back upstairs, then a hand shot out with my clothes. I put them on and switched on my computer. It automatically logged on to my teacher Mrs Curley's computer. I said, 'Good morning, Mrs Curley,' and she said, 'Good morning, Jamie.'

I said hello to Taha, Steven, Josh and Gareth. We did some English and then Mrs Curley said, 'Boys, it's playtime.'

We quickly put on our ear pieces and went outside to play. Fifteen minutes later, the whistle went in our ear pieces and we ran back to the computer. Mrs Curley gave us our spelling and said it was dinner time. In the afternoon we did some Maths, Science and designed a robot. At three o'clock Mrs Curley said, 'Switch off your computers, it's home time. I'll see you tomorrow at nine-thirty. Goodbye.'

Jamie Prosser
Age 7

Illustration by Katie Jones
Age 7

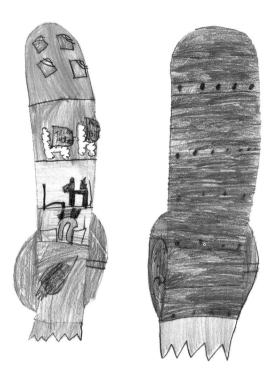

My school is a space rocket. It has a funny door so if you're feeling angry you go through the door with the unhappy face. If you're feeling jolly you go through the door with the smiley face. Year Two have got fluffy seats and the Nursery have got a rocket room!

*Writing and Illustration
by Jenny Atter
Age 7*

We can go to alien school. In alien school, if you are naughty, you go down the mud slide. If you are good, you go to the park.

The alien slug is going to crash into the wall. One of the spiders has been struck by lightning.

You have to be careful in alien school.

*Writing and Illustration by
Christopher Dodd
Age 6*

How about if at school everyone had their own massaging chair. So whenever you felt worn out, you pressed a button and you got a free massage!

Danielle Holmes
Age 8

I think we will have flying shoes. Mine will fly me to school.

Writing and Illustration by
Emily Chitnis
Age 4

I hope that there will be a little girl or boy who does your homework for you. You go into school and collect your work. Then the little person does it. It's a little person who is exactly the same as a human, but who has been shrunk. You would type on the computer if you want one. All you type is your address, then an aircraft comes along and drops one off at your house.

Sarah Neary
Age 8

There will be a robot that can be a teacher. It will have the same looks as an ordinary teacher, but instead of giving the naughty child discipline for getting an answer wrong, it will press a button and an electric shock will go under the carpet of the classroom, up the chair legs, up the naughty child's bum and give them an electric shock. If a child is good, a sweet goes under the carpet, up the child's jumper and pops out in front of them. All this is done just by the teacher pressing buttons on his or her desk.

The robot teacher might blow up and the robot children have to try and fix it. The memory would have changed, so all the teacher said was either, 'You can go outside and play games, stay inside and draw a picture, or go home.'

They all went home.

Josephine Connah
Age 8

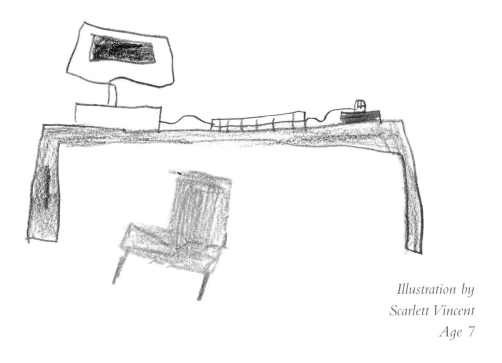

Illustration by
Scarlett Vincent
Age 7

No School in the Millennium

No teachers, no blackboard,
No uniform in the millennium.

Where is the school?
No books, no classroom.

We're on the Internet, my friends and I,
Getting our lessons in the sky.

Writing and Illustration by
Sophie Mulford
Age 8

The Teacher Crusher is a very handy toy for getting rid of teachers. This item includes choppers to chop off teachers' heads, a rifle, a laser, an army of mechanical ants, a saw, a nuclear bomb, an axe and an electric chair.

Writing and Illustration by
James Pye
Age 9

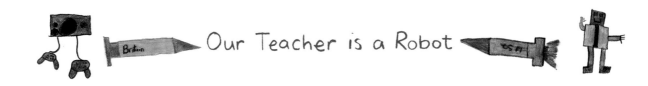

Mega cool school

In the millennium I hope the school will be allowed rock bands at dinner and break and everyone will be allowed a puppy to train instead of lessons.

I hope the school will be free and we can wear whatever we want. I also hope that there is a swimming pool made out of the playground with a space bowl waterslide and loads of steep waterslides to play on. I think the school should be knocked down and made into a Go-Kart course and an amazing 'gunge the teachers' machine (if they get anything wrong they get gunged).

I hope the little ones can have a bouncy castle and a happy magic magician show for them. REAL MEGA.

Writing and Illustration by
Jessica Hughes
Age 9

21st Century School

20th century features
Of a 20th century school.
Are 20th century teachers
20th century cool?

History, Geography, Technology?
After the millennium, what will we see?
Science, Art, Maths, Games and P.E.?
In the new century, what will there be?

Will there be U.F.O.-ology?
Will there be Monster Studies?
Will there be Pluto Geography?
Will we have alien buddies?

Will we have computer pencils?
Will we have day trips to Mars?
Will we have metallic classrooms?
Will there be schools in the stars?

Will there be bouncy playgrounds?
Will we have gravity boots?
Will we have space-age lunch boxes?
Will there be flying suits?

21st century features
Of a 21st century school.
Are 21st century teachers
21st century cool?!

Jessica Gibbs
Age 10

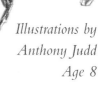

Illustrations by
Anthony Judd
Age 8

There will be no schools. If anybody builds them, they get chucked into jail and the teachers do, too.

Jamie Bradshaw
Age 9

Classroom 2020

No teacher, just a boring robot,
Robot always shouts.
Which is different from Miss Campbell,
Because she's quiet as a mouse.

No jotters, just lap-top computers,
Which always bleep,
No blackboard, just a big TV.
No library, just a computer.

She never tells us anything,
So we never know what to do.
Which is different from Miss Campbell,
Because she tells you what to do.

Illustration by Greg Scott
Age 9

Ross Bell
Age 9

Illustration by
Millie Sharp
Age 6

160

SUBJECT	COMMENTS	MARK
Maths	Jacqueline was good at 2-hour sums. Maybe she can do 9-hour sums.	B+
English	Good autobiography. I liked when the aliens came down.	C+
Science	It was good how she tried to blow up the school.	C+
Space	Jacqueline made super space boots, and they worked.	B
D.T.	Jacqueline made another Titanic and it sank.	C
Drama	Jacqueline was good on *Home and Away*.	B+
Music	Jacqueline made sweet music as she got in the Charts.	B
History	Jacqueline made a time machine, but it blew up in the air.	C

Jacqueline Brown
Age 11

Sometimes normal school chairs are uncomfortable. So I thought of an invisible chair that is the most comfortable chair ever. It can take up as much or as little room as you want. The best thing about this chair is that with a comfortable chair, a child can work better. The bad thing about it is that sometimes you can't see it. But you can leave a jumper on your chair so that you can find it.

Duncan Gammie
Age 11

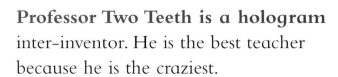

Professor Two Teeth is a hologram inter-inventor. He is the best teacher because he is the craziest.

Writing and Illustration by
Ronan Prior
Age 9

It would be fun if the schools were run by crazy-looking robots instead of teachers, except for Mr Evans.

Rhys James
Age 8

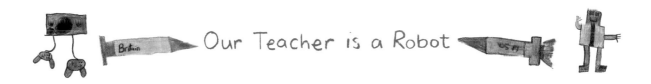

When I grow up I want to be a teacher in secondary school. I would like to teach manners. I will have one child to see what they are like, and if I like them, I will have more children. If I cannot be a teacher I will be a pop star.

Kelly Gill
Age 8

Illustration by
Jennifer May
Age 9

I think that every child will have a computer that they will have lessons on. They will all be connected to each other. Everyone will be on the Internet. All children have to log on in the morning with their teacher. The teacher will set work for each pupil to do as homework. The pupils will start when they want to, and will work for four hours a day, except Saturdays, Sundays and their birthday.

Nimat Naoum
Age 11

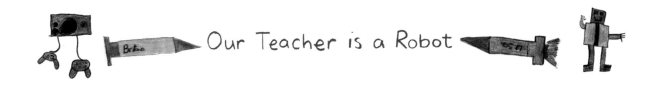
Robin Robot
We have a new teacher in our school.
She looks quite strange, but she's really cool.
Robin Robot is her name,
And making us work is her game!

Lynsey Jones
Age 9

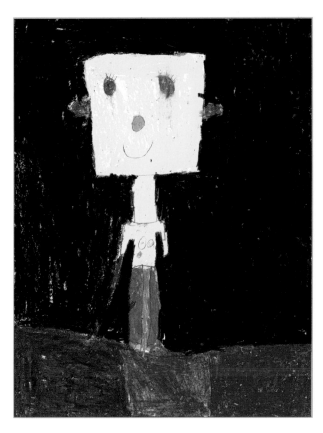

Illustration by
Loren Pey
Age 7

Monday 19th April 2099:
To get to school I travelled on my pet giant mouse, Monty.
Monty is about four feet tall and six feet long. At school the
lessons were just P.E., bullying the teachers and eating rudely.

Abi Meakin
Age 10

In the next century I think school will have been abolished, but when you are born you will have a mini computer inserted inside your head instead of a brain, and under your hair there will be a slot. Every time you go to the doctor, they put a floppy disk in the back of your head so that knowledge is inserted into the computer. You can also play games in your head.

Josh Howell
Age 8

Robot Teacher

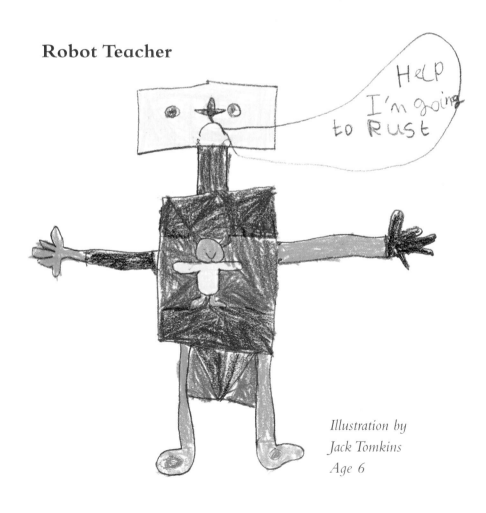

Illustration by
Jack Tomkins
Age 6

If pupils misbehave, they get three chances, and after three chances they have to go to a children's home. For being good for a whole term and finishing all their work at school and finishing their homework, they get £500 as a treat from the school. If they don't want the money, and are good the whole year round, they get a brand new computer at the end of the year.

Jason Clark
Age 10

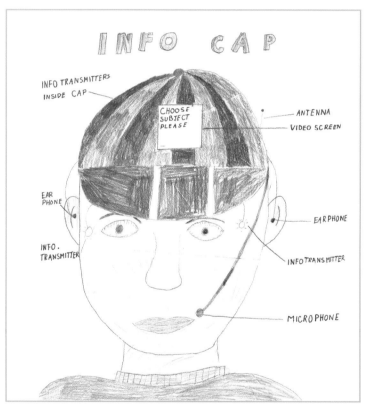

Now you really can put on your thinking cap.
£99.99 isn't much to pay for life-long genius.

Writing and Illustration by
Iain Campbell
Age 11

Flying Cars

and

Hoverboards

Transport

Border illustrations by
Soraya Robinson, Age 9 and
Thomas Clapton, Age 9

You can do anything with a house that flies! And a car which children can drive on the road. You can press a button and OFF WE GO!

All these things will happen in the next millennium and that's what it's all about!

Rachel Anderson
Age 5

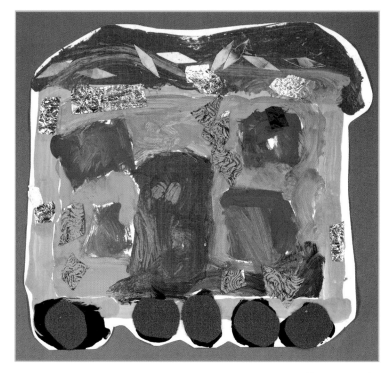

A House Car

Illustration by
Daniel Bailie
Age 4

There will be no more buses and lorries and cars will be gone. People will walk all day and their feet will ache every day.

James Wilman
Age 6

This could be a police vehicle for the year 2000.

Illustration by
Tom McCracken
Age 11

I think in the future cars will have cube-shaped wheels and it will be bumpy.

Writing and Illustration by
Kellie Reaney
Age 5

There will be a little trolley that takes you anywhere you want. It will look like a sofa with drapes that you pull across when you need to go to the toilet. This machine is made of metal and foam and powered by electricity. It would be the size of a table. We can sit in it all day.

These machines can glow in the dark so you can see where you're going. It will make a big difference. No people will be crossing the roads because everyone would have one, poor and rich. There will be no toilets, no houses and no schools because it's so clever. But there will be supermarkets.

Writing and Illustration by
Charlotte Mitchell
Age 7

This is a flying chair, because it goes up in the air. I can go to Majorca and Whitby.

Writing and Illustration by
Holly Theaker
Age 5

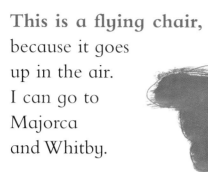

Speed:
999,999,999,
999,999,999,
999,999 miles
per pure-second

Lighting torch, Scanner Radar and target for the laser

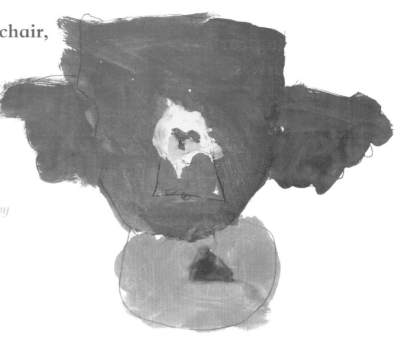

Turbo Zapper
Exterminator

Blow-up road and air wheels

Illustration by
Callum Saxton
Age 8

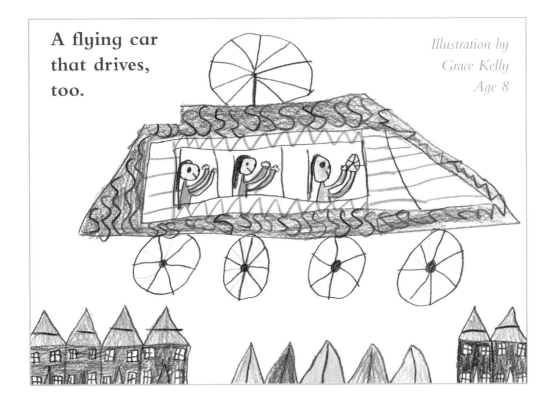

A flying car that drives, too.

Illustration by Grace Kelly Age 8

I think that cars will be different. I would like there to be a dream car. Instead of things like steering wheels, gear sticks, brakes, accelerators or even keys, you simply say 'go' and 'stop'. You just say where you want to go and it goes.

It is not a boring sort of magic car because if you're hungry, it gives you different kinds of meals: dinner, lunch, breakfast, desserts and drinks. A dream car has wings. It can also go in water.

I think maybe aeroplanes will change, too. When I'm older I would like to be an artist or an author. In my spare time, I would like to invent new things.

Hannah Clarke Age 8

We will travel space in starships and explore the unexplored in other dimensions and galaxies. Time machines could take us to different times in the past and in the future. Maybe we will have twenty lives so if we get injured or destroyed we will be able to heal instantly and lose one of our lives and still live.

Money will become history and swapping will become part of life and diseases will no longer be a problem. You will have your own personal forcefield.

I am very hopeful because when we are in the universe floating around, the Earth will regain its strength.

Tim Jones
Age 9

Illustration by Matthew Sparkes
Age 6

In the next millennium we will run out of fossil fuels. Then we will have to find a different way to travel.

For short journeys we could get a dog to pull us on roller skates, or walk. For longer journeys we could get a horse to pull our old car.

If we wanted to go to France by boat we would have six blue whales and six orca whales pulling us along. Altogether that makes twelve whales pulling us.

To travel by air we might get sixty eagles to pull us along. It could be thirty golden and thirty brown ones.

I think to go on a train we would have to get two elephants to pull us along.

Writing and Illustration by
Sian Williams
Age 9

When I Grow Up

Some day when I am older
And own my own sports car,
I'll drive like Ayrton Senna
Up and down the yard.
There'll be no duck nor chicken,
From here to Timbuctoo,
That won't fear the sound of my motor,
Or end up in Mother's stew.
I'll drive around like crazy
In and out the chicane.
With those chickens pushing up daisies
The yard will never be the same.
Burning rubber to the finish
I'll be the first to cross the line.
But for my confirmation pledge
I think I'd try the wine.
If Teacher says to change this verse,
Which I would not do,
If he stepped out in front of my car,
He'd join them chickens, too.

Gary Fealy
Age 12

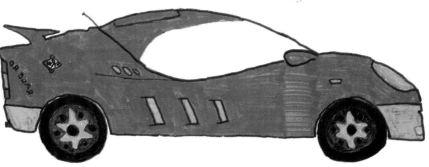

Illustration by
Stephen Mullan
Age 9

The Miniplane

This is the car of the future. Well, sort of. This miniplane is much faster than a car, so it will be easier to get somewhere. It can fly so fast, its maximum speed is 100,006mph! It can only carry one person. It costs 100 pounds. It can go as fast as two million cheetahs put together.

Writing and Illustration by
Sam Lubner
Age 7

Illustration by
Laura Martin-Ward
Age 7

This Lorry Can go over hills faster than other cars and Buses and other Transports

In 100 years' time we might be zooming and rushing around on giant snails with 12 V12 engines on two little feet. They can have as many engines as you want. You have to refill some snails with slime.

You can go to shops and buy them at Snail's the Word or just go on the snail taxi. The snails with fridges and swimming pools and TVs and stereos do cost more, but they are worth it.

They are cute and they have their own name that they respond to. You can get them in any colour. They can do your ironing and housework, cook the food and wash the dishes (they grow little arms to do all this!).

Writing and Illustrations by
Emily McCarthy
Age 11

Illustration by
Jonathan Allcock
Age 5

Illustration by
Joseph Bluck
Age 6

We will have better transport. Finer boats, quicker planes, better cars. But is this all really needed? Isn't the transport of now good enough? Don't our planes go quickly enough? Are the boats not fine and luxurious enough?

If we make more cars we have to think what it will do to our land. If we make more ships, what will it do to our sea? If we make more planes, are we sure this will not affect our ozone layer? We should think for our future children. If we make all of these, what will become of our world?

If we go on making more things, will our world last?

Sara Haddada
Age 11

These wings will make it easier to fly to school if cities are in the air.

Writing and Illustration by
Anthony Purcell
Age 8

Illustration by
Kelly Thomson
Age 5

We will be going on more different holidays not just to the North or South Pole, but to Pluto or Jupiter or some other planets. Or maybe back in time to the Titanic or the Battle of Hastings.

Wouldn't it be cool to see if you were important enough to get a lifeboat to survive the freezing water?

For chocolate lovers, a trip to Cadbury's Chocolate Land so you can eat the lamppost – or maybe you would eat your cat or dog. I will leave you with this thought.

Writing and Illustration by
Kate Edhouse
Age 9

I would recommend for the grandpas a little flying beetle that goes ten miles per hour. For the grannies, a sheltered shopping trolley that goes two miles per hour. For the dads, the smartest Ferrari around that goes 50 zillion miles per hour with power steering, and everything you could possibly want. And for the ladies, well, broom, b–r–o–o–m – crash! Finally, the boys – broom, broom, brooom!

David Taha
Age 11

Zooming Car

Illustration by
Nathan White
Age 10

The car in space
Zoomed to its base
And won the race.

Joshua Miles
Age 6

Travel

Illustration by
Hannah Essam
Age 6

I believe that the pavements should be bigger and us kids should be allowed to ride our bikes on them because the roads are so dangerous. Also it would be great if all cars were run on electricity because the air in the towns and cities would be a lot cleaner.

Rhys James
Age 8

When you ride your bike and it rains you press a rain button and it will turn into a pram. Then someone will start pushing you.

Chris Anderton
Age 8

Illustration by
Bryony Acketts
Age 7

Illustration by Liam Harken
Age 9

We will have to invent a new way to travel because petrol will soon run out, so we might have to invent something called a water-drop car. It will be called a water-drop car because it only needs one drop of water to move. I definitely think this amazing world will be even better, because I think we will stop polluting the air and so all animals can live.

Writing and Illustration by
Alice Lamb
Age 7

For the millennium I have done a car. It's a special car because it has not got any wheels. It's got these hover things that make the car move. And it's got video camera headlights so they can film cars going by.

But that's not all. There is a lever instead of a steering wheel, so even blind people can drive it. On my picture you can see there are some wires. Those are only to make the hover things work. So you can see how long it took me to do my picture.

Writing and Illustration by
Charles Wade
Age 8

Wires that make the hover things work.

Things that make the car hover along.

Video camera headlights

The hover car is designed to go through buildings.
It has a rocket booster and a bullet-proof body. The car has a programmer which you can use to tell it where to go and it takes you there. The name of the hover car is Road Kill. In the future I think we will be green.

Writing and Illustration by
James Jardine
Age 11

In the year 2000 we will have kiddie cars.
They will be fuelled by pineapple juice. You will buy them for £100 and they will look like a Ferrari, but mini versions.

Writing and Illustration by
Phoebe Coleman
Age 9

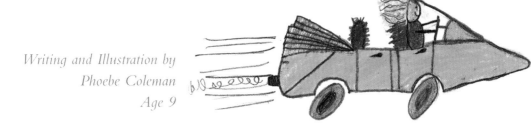

Illustration by
Hannah Craggs
Age 10

In the next millennium we will be walking on the ceilings.
And we will be travelling in our houses. We will be flying without
hoverboards. We will have automatic pencils so we won't have to
do our homework. We will have automatic doors so that we don't
have to open them. And we will have a new day called Funday.
We will have terminators to guard us from killers.

   The bit I am looking forward to is the houses moving in the
air, so we end up in different countries each week.

Paul Hanson
Age 7

There is now a new type of transport in Aberdeen which is called the Aberdeen Monorail. Everone has to park their cars in the carparks and take the Monorail into the city centre. This stops the amount of pollution going into the city.

Writing and Illustration by
Daniel Hendry
Age 9

Police Patrol Unit

Illustration by
Theo Fitzharris
Age 8

The Flying Tractor

The flying tractor can fly from one field to another using its wings. The plough has swords. The swords spin round and round, digging up the ground. The laser gun can zap very big stones.

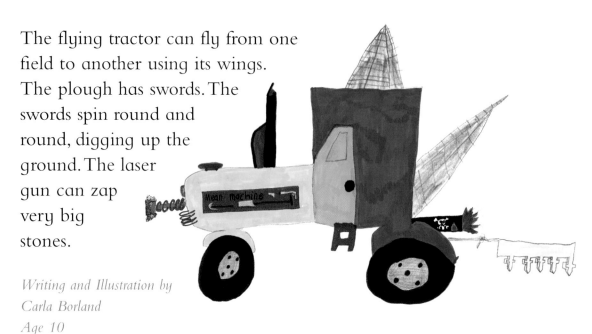

*Writing and Illustration by
Carla Borland
Age 10*

If people could fly, that would be good. We could wear a special suit and when you press a button you go up in the air.

*Writing and Illustration by
Amy Saunders
Age 9*

T-Shirts Made of Goo

Looks and Fashion

Border illustrations by
Sophie Henley
Age 10

People will have teeth that stick out, with the best big ears that can hear ants crawling about.

You can make your eyes move forward, but the white bit stays in your head. You can see through walls with these new eyes.

You can get every answer right with a brain that is also used to play games like chess, Scrabble, chequers, draughts and many more.

Your fingers can grow up to 30 feet long. You can make them grow any time you want them to.

Your nose can smell things up to 200 miles away. You can be much better at smelling than your dog.

If you like football, with your excellent hands you can save high goals! Your feet can reach 69 miles, so you can just stay in defence while your foot scores a goal.

With your trendy hair you can do a lot of things. You can push it in without going to the hairdresser. You can listen to the radio on the cool radar systems in your head. You can be as narrow as string or very dumpy.

Illustration by
Becky Church
Age 5

Adam Davies
Age 9

Spacesuits made of tinfoil

Spacesuits made of tinfoil,
Hats of rubber bands.
Hair done up in tight coils,
Thick gloves for your hands.
Platform shoes with plastic soles,
Metal tights with great big holes.
That's millennium!

Ride a big wheel to the moon.
Won't be long – I'll be back soon.
Have a penpal up on Mars –
Lots and lots of chocolate bars!
Ride along the Milky Way.
It will only take a day.
That's millennium!

Kerry Sadler
Age 9

Illustrations by
Mollie Winward
Age 11

By the year 3000 we might all be wearing three-foot-high platform boots to keep us above the rubbish that litters our Earth. Breathing masks and fish-bowl helmets will be worn when we go outside to protect us from the air pollution. Special thin silver suits will protect us from the merciless sun.

Sophie Volhard
Age 8

Fashion in the year 2300

In the year 2300, fashion will depend on what people do and the weather. People will have more leisure time, so clothes will be very decorative with flashing lights and bright colours.

It will probably be a lot warmer because of global warming, so clothes will have to be light and cool. They will be made out of special materials that keep out the sun's rays. Most clothes will be disposable, as people will not want to wash them and water will not be so plentiful.

Illustration by Jessica Hogg Age 6

Special clothes will be cleaned by a spray. People will spend more time inside because of heat and pollution outside. Whole cities will be under cover, so people will shop and do business by computer at home, so they will keep cleaner.

Hard or dirty work will be done by robots or worker-people. It will not be important for them to look good, so they will wear one-piece grey overalls.

Important people will wear loose, casual clothes in gold or silver material. For holidays, people will buy clothes in a can which are sprayed on each morning and washed off in a special shower.

Lydia Shaw Age 9

 192

In the year 2000 we will have posh clothes with streaked shiny sparkles of glitter, furry collars and loads of leather and loads of inventions for make-up, for instance one that you could put under your neck like a perfume made out of bubble bath and herbs, like a lavender smell with a hint of camomile and a bit, just a bit, of tea tree. I think that's a herb. You could call it Peach of Flowers.

Zara Fernandez
Age 8

Illlustration by
Lauren Gornall
Age 4

I think there will be lots of punks. I think most of the other people will have classic fashion. Men will wear suits like in the old films. Ladies will wear dresses like in old films.

Robert Baker
Age 8

CHAZZA   DIKA   FREEKA

Illustrations by
Nicole Hunt
Age 11

We might have different hair styles, like we might wear plaits and clip them up with clips. We might have four pigtails and hold them up with a pencil. You might have different clothes: you might have a dress that has sunflowers and butterflies popping out of it.

Writing and Illustration by
Natalie, Age 8
Laurencekirk Primary School

I think the ladies will wear short skirts made from imitation fur, half tops and high heels. Their hair will be in punk style, the colours of the rainbow. They will carry a mobile phone with two screens, one to show who is talking to them. The other will be a small television screen.

Rosalind Parkinson
Age 12

Illustrations by
Charlotte Carney
Age 10

For boys there will be trousers that look like boot legs and T-shirts made of goo because some boys like goo. But some boys don't like goo so they have normal T-shirts.

Kayleigh Ventum
Age 7

THE MILLENNIUM GIRL!

PRICE
£50.00

Disco Dancing Dress
The silver dress with mini CDs all over. Get it from all designer stores. For the millennium girl.

Price: £2,500

Hat
Disco dancing hat with green antennae. Also with mini CDs all over.

Price: £2,050

Price: £2,000

Boots
CD boots. The high-heel shoe in fashion. Your friends will be jealous of you.

Writing and Illustrations by Lauren Wood Age 10

Brilliant Fashion

I think we will wear a long, thin dress with very long, thin high heels, and to go with the dress a silver cape to keep us a bit warmer. Dresses could have sleeves or no sleeves. If they don't have sleeves, you could wear some very nice gloves with fur around them, because fur is very good in fashion. Fashion is excellent. Fashion is very, very good. You could have fur on your dress, on your cape, on your gloves. There are lots of places where fur can go.

Writing and Illustration by
Jessica Riggall
Age 8

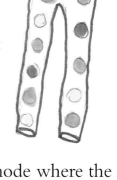

We will have a marvellous high-tech gold switch on our trousers and have safety wire down to all these fabulously coloured lights. But these are no ordinary light bulbs, these are very special ones – you never ever have to change them! There are three different modes: a flashing mode where you can change how many seconds in between each flash. Another mode where the lights stay on, and another one where you can make it do stripes. When it's hot they keep you cool, and when it's cold they keep you warm.

Writing and Illustration by
Laura Turner
Age 10

197

There will be all sorts of people wearing all sorts of clothes. Teachers might even go to work dressed as a vegetable. Children will be dressed as people on the catwalk. Grown-ups that work in offices will wear party clothes or clown suits. Our everyday clothes will look like we're aliens that have just landed on Earth from Mars.

Writing and Illustrations by
Rosie Simpson
Age 9

We will have blue and white hair. We will all have to wear pretty dresses, even the boys.

We will have silver eyes, a motley-coloured body, horns sticking out of our heads and pointed ears like Dumbo.

Writing and Illustrations by
Shelley Davies
Age 8

Every piece of clothing is made out of scraps, so these clothes do not cost a lot to make and they use recycled materials:

- Pencils used as hair rollers
- Paper-clips used as a necklace
- Belt made out of calculators
- Dress with eight zips
- Shoes made out of cardboard

Writing and Illustration by
Kate Bailey
Age 9

We will be nicer and our faces won't have spots or freckles and our noses won't be big. The jobs will be better than they are just now. You won't do anything but sit down and let the machines do it, while you are eating doughnuts and you get paid £399 for doing nothing.

Andrew Shaw
Age 11

Illustration by
Evelyn Battye
Age 7

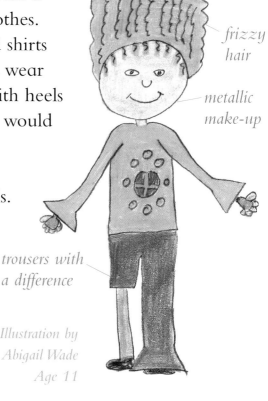

frizzy hair

metallic make-up

trousers with a difference

We could look like Elvis, with a funky hair style and funky clothes. Boys would wear hipsters and shirts with frilly sleeves. Girls would wear pretty little colourful frocks with heels the size of a 30cm ruler. Boys would wear high heels as well.

No more tracksuit and trainers – all hipsters and heels. Everyone would walk about like Elvis with a guitar or a drum. It's just the way it is.

Ashleigh Burns
Age 11

Illustration by
Abigail Wade
Age 11

There will be no fashion, we will all wear the same. The clothes will be like uniforms, warm in winter, cool in summer. They will probably be electronic so that we can talk to anyone in the world at any time.

Sarah Thomas
Age 8

I think in the future we will all be couch potatoes. We will sit inside all day, watching television and stuffing our faces with crisps. It will not be a pretty sight.

The way we speak would probably be affected, too, and we would mumble and talk slang. There would be no school or jobs, as computers would do our work for us, so we would never have to leave the house except to stock up on junk food.

I wouldn't be surprised if future children are born without any legs, as they will have no use for them.

I do hope our world will not become home to unhealthy couch potatoes. We must do all we can to stop this becoming true before it is too late.

Teri Polson
Age 11

casual

wedding

Illustrations by
Natalie Stocker
Age 8

Facial Expressions

Normally, if you were happy or sad, your face would just change shape, e.g. if you were happy your mouth would go up, and if you were sad your mouth would go down.

In the year 2000, if you are happy your face will go yellow. To find out more, look at the list of colours and expressions below, and prepare to get colourful:

Happy	Yellow
Sad	Purple
Crying	Blue
Frightened	White
In Love	Red
Angry	Brown
Lonely	Green
Excited	Pink
Surprised	Orange

Chloë Hughes
Age 10

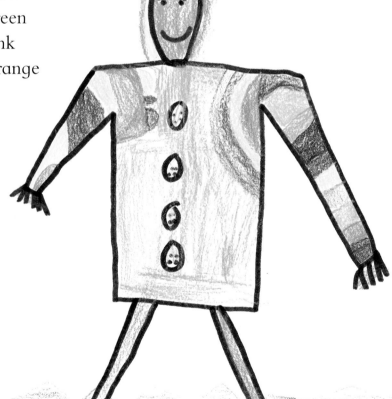

Illustration by
Kerry-Anne Lee
Age 5

We will not have long hair.
Everyone's hair will be short.
There will be no lipstick.
There will be green contact lenses.
Tights will be extinct.

David Baines
Age 9

Illustration by
Charlotte Jenkyn
Age 8

The police may be wearing blue and green shirts, but Santa would still be wearing red on his head. People could be wearing a mini skirt for a top. Trousers may be short and shorts may be long. There might be colourful clothes or dark clothes. Children may be wearing purple for school. If people were walking with someone daft, they would have 'fool' on their shirts.

Natalie Ellis
Age 9

We will wear hats that are crowns with gems glittering like stars in the sunlight. Our coats will be long like a king's. Girls will wear plain, dull clothes.

Philip Whitehead
Age 8

Clothes will be outrageous. I will wear sequined yellow high-as-a-shelf shoes and red sequined shorts and black sequined crop tops. The teachers will wear tight army dresses and high-heeled shoes.

Kleary Vasquez
Age 9

Illustrations by
Sophie Henley
Age 10

I think in the 21st century men will be wearing make-up to make them look more attractive. I also think men will enjoy wearing make-up, and they will have a little compact pouch to keep their make-up in.

People will be wearing really glamorous, glitzy clothes, even for just walking down the street. Children will probably dress like their parents.

I think people's fashion and looks are going to be weird and wacky. Punks and other people will be really outrageous, like instead of getting a part of your ear or nose pierced, you'll get a part of your head done.

Now, for our dear grandparents. What they really need is to look younger, so I thought maybe in the 21st century there might be a cream to make old people look 20 years younger.

Hollie Begg
Age 10

Illustration by
Paul Schoolar
Age 11

The Sheep-Patterner Gun

This invention works by pointing the sheep-patterner gun at a sheep. Then choose from 1,000 different designs and just click the button which says 'press'. A laser comes out and automatically makes a pattern on the sheep's fleece. Then you shear the sheep and make it into a coat (you can use it on jumpers as well).

Writing and Illustration by
Harriet Karwatowska
Age 11

Men Will Have Babies

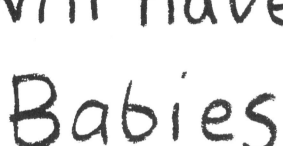

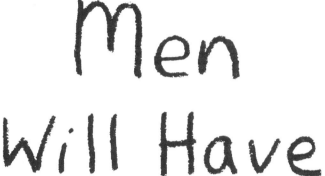

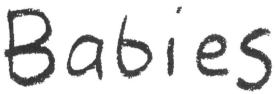

My Family, My Friends and Me

Border illustrations by
Annabelle Price
Age 8

Designer Babies

I think people in the next millennium can have designer babies. You could choose what kind of personality you want your child to have and the colour of eyes you want them to have. You could even choose the colour of hair, from black to orange. It's your choice.

Maybe you could decide whether you want your child to be tall, medium or short. If scientists in the future are clever enough, they could even control or estimate what age and date your baby is going to die, or maybe the date you want your baby to be born.

Maybe a few thousand years later, scientists might come up with a screen to picture what your child is going to look like when he or she grows up.

Mumtaz Begum
Age 10

Micro–Babe

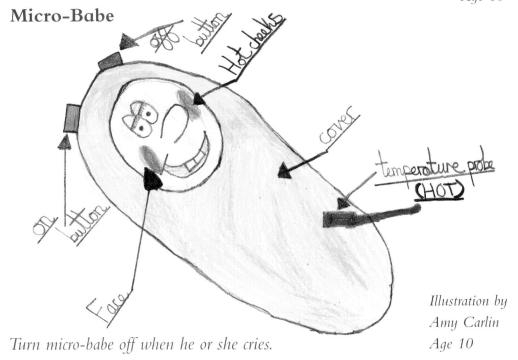

Turn micro-babe off when he or she cries.

Illustration by
Amy Carlin
Age 10

Funky Mum

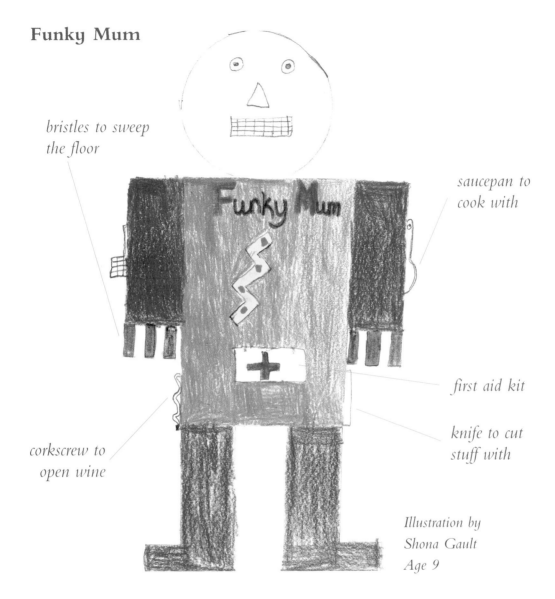

bristles to sweep the floor

saucepan to cook with

first aid kit

corkscrew to open wine

knife to cut stuff with

Illustration by Shona Gault Age 9

I think there will be robots. They will be like mums, but a little bit better, because they might be able to do three things at once.

My mummy can only do one thing at once. I want my mum to do six things at once. That would be good.

Kirsty Butler
Age 8

I would like to have an invention called the baby chooser, so you can choose what kind of baby you would like, a girl or a boy, blue eyes, green eyes, brown eyes or hazel eyes, a small baby, a big baby or a medium-sized baby. If I were a mummy, I would have a good baby and I would care for her.

Houses would have a robot to clean them, so mums, brothers and sisters could be lazy and sit and watch telly or play upstairs or at the park or play at home with Lego.

Alexandra Lumby
Age 6

Illustration by
Jade Smalley
Age 7

I would love to be able to order a new brother or sister in a catalogue, and send them back to the store when they get boring! I wish I could have a baby sister who stayed the same age.

Terri Spearritt
Age 10

Illustration by
Victoria Houston
Age 4

A family made out of metal playing in their house. Six robots playing games and one left over outside.

Writing and Illustration by
Jamie Brock
Age 6

In the year 2018 I will be 25 years old. I will not want children out of my belly. I will be a teacher. I will be a kind teacher. I will marry Nicholas Slater. Nicholas and me love each other.

Writing and Illustration by
Emma Carmody
Age 6

Illustration by
Kate O'Dowda
Age 5

We should not fall out with our friends, because they are very important to us and they are always there when we need them, and they never let us down. Don't bully other people, because they might just bully you back some day.

If people loved each other like themselves, the world would be a much kinder and better place to live.

Victoria Hargreaves
Age 8

I think me and Lucy and Rachel will live together.

Illustration by
Katie Mulholland
Age 5

I wish I could have a holiday at the space zoo.
I would see fat aliens, small aliens, tall aliens, little aliens and normal aliens. I could sneak different kinds, so I could take them home.
    If any alien robber came, they could stick their tongues out at them and they would run away down a hole in the planet.
    If my mummy or daddy came up to my bedroom, the aliens would sink into the floor and creak.
    I would have a robot that mummy and daddy knew about. It would fold my clothes, wash the floor and make my bed, which would be good.

James Wilkinson
Age 7

Illustrations by
Daniel Farrell
Age 4

They might invent something to make my mummy younger.

Writing and Illustration by
Kori Beard
Age 5

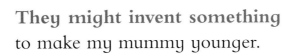

I will still love my mum in the year 2000. I hope that Mrs Hyden will still be my teacher in the year 2000.

Gurpreet Nijjar
Age 12

I will be a mummy and I will have children. And I will be a vet and I will make animals better.

Lizzie Wlodarczyk
Age 5

Illustration by Nicholas Caley
Age 4

Some families will have about twenty identical children because they could clone them.

Chiara Pelizzari
Age 9

Illustration by Fiona Walley
Age 8

Men Will Have Babies

People will be bigger than they think.

Writing and Illustration by Rachel Ford Age 6

Dad as he is.　　*Dad as he was.*

I think there will be aliens and E.T. living on Earth, and we will be able to learn things from the aliens and E.T., and they will be able to learn things from us. They will be able to have driving lessons, and we will be able to have spaceship lessons. We could go to their planet if we passed our spaceship lessons, and they could go to our planet for a week. They could be our friends. They would be mummy-shaped, then you could hug them when you're sad. They would be very cheerful, and the aliens and E.T. would be very happy.

Bethany Foley, Age 6

Illustration by Joel Scully, Age 5

we ARe ALiens !

 215

Illustration by Joseph Steer
Age 9

In the year 2000 I will probably look like a secret agent in a black suit. Or maybe I will be heard on the radio. I might be a singer or an actor.

What I really want to be is a secret agent. I would like to make lots of money and buy a huge mansion with three floors. I would like to buy a limo, too.

But I don't think I will be rich.

Kenneth Buckley
Age 9

Maybe men will have babies and give babies breast milk.

I think that martians will be our friends. Everyone's made of rubber. Girls are bald. Newest fashion might be being naked. Everyone will have their own special power. Men will have big breasts.

Megan Alderton
Age 7

Illustration by
Susan Samson
Age 11

The Marriage Machine

How to Marry:

1 Put in 20p.
2 Put in birth certificates.
3 Use the touch-sensitive keypad to say your marriage vows and select a honeymoon.
4 Enjoy the sights and sounds of your video honeymoon on the screen and with the headphones.
5 Wait for your marriage certificate to come out from the printer and insert your finger into the finger holes and two rings will be provided.
6 Sign the marriage certificate and confetti will be blown out of the confetti hole.

confetti hole

honeymoon video

money slot

finger hole

touch-sensitive keyboard pad

pencil to sign marriage certificates

headphones to hear sounds from the place you want to go on your honeymoon

finger hole

printer to print wedding certificates

slot for birth certificates

How to Divorce:

1 Press the divorce button.
2 Type your names into the divorce keypad and the machine will retract your marriage.
3 Put your rings and marriage certificates into the divorce slot.

divorce touchpad

divorce slot

divorce button

Writing and Illustration by
Kate Pearson
Age 11

Men Will Have Babies

When I grow up, I think I will look similar to how I look now, because I have reddy-coloured hair which does not normally change colour very much, but I might grow a moustache like my dad's.

I think houses will be the same as they are now except for the size of the gardens, which will be a lot smaller because there will not be as much space in the world. People will have jobs that use computers more, and we will come to rely on these machines more and more, which will make our lives better, because we will be able to spend more time on holiday activities or playing football or swimming.

I hope a lot of this comes true because I would like to spend the early part of my grown-up life playing football.

Jonathan Breeze
Age 7

Illustration by Sarah Langston
Age 9

218

When I grow up I will be able to fly on a wishing chair into sweetie land.

Writing and Illustration by
Olivia Morton
Age 6

In the future I might travel in an aeroplane and have lots of fun. I might grow bigger and do more things. It will be more exciting and much better for me. I could read better by writing the words down, like the word 'frightened'. I will care for and help more people as the years go by.

I might find a boat and sail it across the river. I might choose someone to come with me. It might be all dusty, so I could paint it. I won't change my mind, but if it is dusty, I will paint it red.

Rachel Banham
Age 6

Towns will be on ships

Illustration by
David Woods
Age 9

Illustration by
Amy Weild
Age 6

Me After the Millennium

I wish there was a slide around my flat.
I wish I had a gunge machine.
I wish I had a spaceship of my own.
I wish I could run as fast as 70 mph
I wish I could have a big playroom
Even bigger than the city, with loads of toys.
I wish I was rich.
I wish I was an eagle.
I wish I was unstoppable.
I wish I was famous.
I wish I was the king of the world.
I wish I was a robot.

Ben Jordan
Age 9

My toy is a millennium teddy bear. She can speak and cry. She loves to dance. When she gets angry, she kicks.

The best thing about her is, when I'm bored, she plays with me.

Writing and Illustration by
Georgina Muir
Age 7

I am going to be a policeman when I grow up and I am going to wear a triangle hat and I will wear a red top.

Writing and Illustration by
Matthew Cawley
Age 5

People

People are nice.
Especially old people are nice.
I like old people.
I love old people.

Jamie Edwards
Age 7

In the next millennium I want to be a party animal. I will build my own house with a swimming pool and a disco. I will invite all of my friends and they can live with me. I will buy them some cool clothes and cool hats.

Jamie Barrett
Age 7

My dad will have a job as a spaceman. That will mean my dad is a substitute for the super Buzz Aldrin, or any other spaceman. My mum will be a school teacher and teach year six for a long time, maybe for ever and ever and ever. My sister will work in a shop called 'Joe's Grub', and be rich like my mum and dad. We will feed the poor and homeless, and give a little money to them. I will work at being a millionaire and a footballer in my spare time.

John Gomez
Age 9

Illustration by
Luke Fuller
Age 10

I am going to be a princess. I am going to be in a very shiny dress with shiny shoes. I will go out to pick sunflowers.

Writing and Illustration by
Heather Gittins
Age 5

My favourite toy would be a teddy that talks. Its name would be Ted and it would sing 'Old MacDonald Had a Farm'.

Writing and Illustration by
Megan Laird Hughes
Age 7

More children, when they are young, would be thinking of being something like a vet or a model or a designer or a pop star. Fewer children would think of being a doctor or a scientist. Teenagers, when about 15, would start a job, e.g. as a paper boy/girl, a cleaner, or in a small shop.

Jennifer Yip
Age 8

Robot Police Officer

claw to grip criminals with

Robot Fireman

stilts so they don't need ladders

Robot Scientist

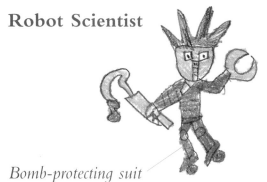

Bomb-protecting suit

Robot Dentist

pliers

I want to be a dentist. I will live in a bungalow and I will be rich. I will get married and have three children. I will make my children happy because I will take them to the circus.

Naveen Shukla
Age 7

Illustrations by
Adam Carter
Age 10

When I am ten years old I am going to be a newspaper boy. And after university I am going to have a few jobs. I am going to be a footballer, a palaeontologist, a doctor, a fireman and a scientist.

As a footballer I would make Tottenham Hotspur win every single cup there is. When I'm playing for Tottenham, I'm going to score 3,200,000,607,346,013 goals, hopefully. I am going to try my best.

As a scientist I am going to make a medicine, a secret medicine, that makes people bald. I can't wait till the future, can you?

Adam Alexander
Age 8

When I am older, I will work for Santa. I will be making toys. I will do whatever Santa tells me. I will tell Santa when to go. I will be invisible. I will live in Lapland. I will be little.

James Philpott
Age 6

Illustration by
Corrin Hornsby-Shawe
Age 5

The President's 'To Do' List

☑ Welcome ceremony for Gorns
(be sensitive, they've travelled 600 light years)

☑ Attend 'Peace Around the World' meeting

☑ Break champagne bottle on Pluto probe

☑ Complimentary facial touch-up from Beautician's Guild

☑ View nuclear disarmament demonstration

☑ Release 4,000 pandas into wild with Our Earth Our Life

☑ Pay off tabloids for incriminating pictures with a Gorgon

☑ Accept a star from the Galactic Alliance Committee

☐ Attend husband's birthday party

Kristen Stegemoeller
Age 11

I will look like a princess.
I will live in a tent. I will work
in McDonald's. I will travel in
a car. I will eat carrots.

Writing and Illustration by
Eloise Morris
Age 6

Ball

Holidays on the Moon

Ball

Ball

Sport and Leisure

Ball

Ball

Border illustrations by
Craig Dewar
Age 11

Ball

People will want to get things done quickly, so ladies might have a make-up gun and a man can shoot the ladies with it and they go out with their make-up on. You have a

spray and you spray it on your nails and they will be done.

You can go on holiday in a car with wings. Instead of eight hours, it would be eight seconds to get there, to save time to do things.

Our houses will be very big, and every house will have a money-making machine.

Scarlett Vincent
Age 7

Illustration by
Liam Briggs
Age 11

The millennium will be great. You can jump into your TV and be in the land of dreams. Yes! So if you are watching *The Simpsons*, you can jump in and say, 'Hello, Homer,' and he will say, 'Doh!' and strangle you a bit.

Philip Whitehead
Age 8

The ultimate drink

As I zoom up the road
On my fire-blazing rollerskates
I see
John, sucking a fizz-up.
Oh, don't you know what they are?
Well, just look.
He's up in the air!
Wheeee . . .
AHHH! Duck!
Here comes Lucy in her flybug.
Look at her, whizzing around.
All those coloured buttons.
They're too confusing for me.
I prefer
The ultimate drink.
You take one sip
And you slowly rise up
Into the clouds.

Writing and Illustration by
Rose Grundy
Age 10

Illustration by
Claire Walsh
Age 10

Breakdown!

The noise of the wind flying past the rocket echoed like the roaring sea. Sam complained to Dad. 'Why do we have to go on holiday to Venus? Why can't we go to Pluto like normal families?'

'Because we aren't *normal*. Everyone is different,' said Dad.

'Both of you shut up,' shouted Mum, ending the argument.

The roar of the engine sounded like a Formula 1 car zooming through space.

Suddenly the engine stuttered and came to a halt.

'What's happened?' said Leroy, waking from his sleep. He was aware of the sudden jolt as the rocket stopped. The engine had broken.

Dad quickly put on his 'Ultra Protective Micro Spacesuit', as the advertisers called it. It was a spacesuit, in other words.

Illustration by
Aneesh Kalra
Age 8

He got the engine working eventually, after a lot of grunting and panting. He used the gluing laser because the side of the spaceship had come off.

'We are on our way to Venus!' shouted Dad.

When we got there we were greeted by an alien. We had a wonderful holiday. We dug for rock as a souvenir. When we were going home we planned our holiday next year, to Saturn.

Louise Davies
Age 10

Illustration by
Oliver Drake
Age 8

'Ladies and gentlemen, thank you for coming tonight. Now this piece of technology is called the hoverboard. As you can see it has different kinds of belts. They go round your feet.

'Please may I have a volunteer from the audience? Errm. Yes, you at the back with the white T-shirt. If you would kindly step onto the stage and then onto the board. If I press the button underneath the board it will hover. You can control the movements of the board or you can put it on automatic. You can get off the board now.

'Remember: always press the button on the bottom of the board when you have finished with it. I will be hoping to make other hover vehicles later on in the decade like buses, cars, taxis, motorbikes, scooters and lorries.

'Thank you and goodnight.'

Jack Stevens
Age 9

Ball

Holidays on the Moon

Illustration by
Frances Hughes
Age 6

People will have more holidays. They will go to America for fun. It will take about half an hour to get to America from England and the people will like it. They will play in the sea. They will wear special clothes so they will stay for a long time under the sea and watch the fishes.

Writing and Illustration by
Iman Adam
Age 9

Fishing will be very advanced. I would like to invent a very highly equipped fishing rod with an automatic reel-in when you have caught a fish. You have a little gun to stick the weight or float in and then you shoot it out to help you cast. I would like to make a new kind of bait that a fish couldn't resist.

When it rains you can blow up a little tent for shelter. If we are not careful pollution will cause fish to become extinct. You should not over-fish but only bring two home.

I think they should stock up the lochs every week so you can catch something in every cast. There may be a cross-breed between species like brown trout and salmon. It will weigh about 50 pounds and be about two metres long. It would be a good idea to have a little pike fishery at the side of the loch in case you get bored.

Writing and Illustration by
Ross Marshall
Age 10

Holidays on the Moon

We will soon be able to get holidays to the moon.
A moon bus will come and pick you up in every big
town. You will manage to ride
on shooting stars. In the
craters you can buy
postcards and tickets for
space fares. You can
do this by wearing a
special suit that keeps
your feet firmly on
the moon and helps
you breathe.

Writing and Illustration by
Danielle Cooper
Age 7

Illustration by
Joshua Flatman,
Age 8

Ball

Holidays on the Moon

In the year 2728 I think the world will be ruled by robots. The boy robots will go out drinking beer and playing football and rugby and will go to hot sunny places, whereas the girls will live in the kitchen preparing food and drink and all that stuff. They will never go to hot places or do any of the things that the men do.

Writing and Illustration by
Jonathan Gillon
Age 9

If you have a football T-shirt on and you go to a football match, you get in free and you play the next match. If you score a goal you join the team.

Jamie Bradshaw
Age 9

I think that we will have robot referees in all games, so they can't take sides, which will make the game fairer.

Writing and Illustration by
Thomas Lovell
Age 10

   236

One day my dad bought a mobile phone. I tried it and magic came sparkling out of it. When I saw the sparkles coming out, I ran up to my room and dialled a number. The phone told me it was Ronan Keating's number, so I called him and asked him for his autograph and a ticket to go and see Boyzone. He sent them to me and I kept them away safe.

Illustration by Lorna Dawson Age 8

On 8th May I went to the concert and I enjoyed it. When I got home I dialled a different number and it was Leonardo DiCaprio. I realised that it was always famous people who were answering. First Ronan Keating and then Leonardo DiCaprio! I was surprised. I started phoning famous people all the time and I gave some of my friends a go and they came over all the time.

Then it was time to pay the bill – it was £2,000! My mum and dad were mad and told me to save up my tuck money.

Jade O'Donnell
Age 10

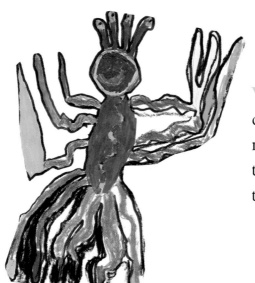

When I go on holiday and I go skiing my teacher may be a ski monster! So the monster might say, 'Put twelve skis on!'

Writing and Illustration by
Jade Tyrer
Age 6

I think people will play in space.
In space I think they will take their dogs and cats.
I think they will wear space clothes.

Damien Smith
Age 6

Illustration by Richard Leeming
Age 7

They will have a new medicine and it will make
footballers be brilliant, especially beginners. It will make
footballers score 85 goals in a match, especially people like
David Johnson and Dwight Yorke. I really want it to happen in
a thousand years' time so my two favourite teams will win.
But I only want it to go to Ipswich Town players and
Manchester United players and I want them to have bright
new football kits so you don't get bored with the same kit all
the time.

Edwin Frost
Age 8

A Football Stadium of the Millennium

Hello. My name is Mushy Mopeledop and I am standing just outside the Universe Cup Stadium where Earth and Mars are playing. Earth are winning 19-0.

They are not playing with an old-fashioned round ball, of course. They are playing with a super-duper Electronic Triball.

The stadium is an octagon-shape. The goals are not the old boring rectangular-shaped goals. They are new and improved diamond-shaped goals. They are an improvement because diamond goals are harder to score and the players shout out the direction for the goalkeeper to go in.

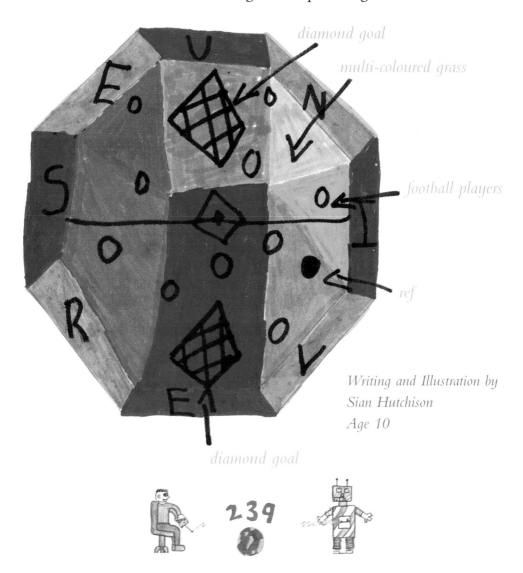

diamond goal

multi-coloured grass

football players

ref

Writing and Illustration by
Sian Hutchison
Age 10

diamond goal

The Football House
Illustration by
Gordon, Age 10
Mid Calder Primary School

The England football team should buy players from Italy and Brazil. They should buy Del Piero, Ronaldo, Inzaghi, Taffarel and Peruzzi. It is very weird, because the people who play for England try harder in the Premiership League.

Kevin Keegan should not give them as much money as he does. When England win a couple of matches then they can get as much money as they do now. If they don't get as much money they might play better to get more money.

Ryan Cumbers
Age 9

Imagine if the world was so small and legs were all you saw. And we could swim through the legs in the pool.

Imagine if you had a ball in your hand and you threw it, and it landed on somebody's head! Imagine if there was a balloon in the sky and there was water inside it – and it popped on someone's head!

What we could do is go on a rocket and take our balloons with us and throw them down. Imagine if you could fly around the world and never ever come back ever again.

Lorrell Sykes
Age 8

Every football manager will receive five billion pounds each year. Ballet will not be permitted. If you are a nurse or doctor, these will be bad years for you. There will be 700 patients each day and one billion each year.

David Baines
Age 9

Change Legs

In the year 2000 I will be a ballet dancer
Change legs, change legs, change legs.
I will go on shows in front of millions of people
Change legs, change legs, change legs.
I will do ballet in front of old people
Change legs, change legs, change legs.
Then I will teach people my changing legs
Change legs, change legs, change legs.

Illustration by
Sarah Crocker
Age 8

Tamisa Worthington
Age 8

Robot Footy!

Michael Owen, David Beckham, Ryan Giggs . . .
I don't think so! Now, new and exclusive . . .
ROBOT FOOTY! All new players. All new
action. I mean, this is more exciting than
the TITANIC!

   Tune in and see David Beckbot and
Ryan Thing-a-majig! If you miss it,
you're roboting crazy!

Writing and Illustration by
Katie Wood
Age 10

Football 2901

The stadium will gleam with glory,
The crowd will be raving mad,
The ref will wear pink Barbie socks,
It really will be bad.

The players will all wear luminous kits,
Their boots fluorescent green,
The cheer leaders wearing matching skirts –
A real sight to be seen!

The linesmen will carry M16s
To shoot any players offside,
The goalies will wear big green gloves
To save any shots that come high.

The goals will be painted a bright, bright orange,
Easy for attackers to see.
The sidelines will all be painted red,
And so will the referee.

The manager will sit on a bouncy castle
Just bouncing, not watching the game.
The subs will run round like lunatics –
They definitely will be insane.

If this is really going to happen
In 2901,
Then I'm really, really, really glad
That I will then be gone!

Writing and Illustrations by
Daniel Kelsall
Age 11

People would be able to visit the other eight planets as holidays. On each planet there would be a hotel with swimming pools and other activities. To get to the planets you would have to ride fast Space Wagons or Space Hoppers.
If you went to Mars, as you left the vehicle you would be given a free Mars Bar with the slogan: A Mars Bar a day keeps the Martian doctor away!

There would be lots of restaurants on the planets, e.g. Starvin' Martians, McAliens (a branch on every planet).

McAliens would serve:
McEyeballs
U.F.O. Burgers
Alien Fingers and
Martian Fries

You may be thinking this will never happen next year, but remember that a millennium is a thousand years, so it may happen later on.

Rachel Sheldon
Age 9

Illustrations by
Sandip Kaur
Age 6

In the years 2020–2040 there will be no football. The whole sport will be taken over by robots. There will be people in a room controlling the robots. Everyone will get fat because robots would do everything so there would be no need for humans. No one would get paid for work because robots would do it for you. The whole world would die.

No football, no golf, no basketball, in fact no sport. Just lazy people sitting at home eating burgers and drinking beer. It would be terrible if this happened. Nothing would be like it is now. I am sure you don't want no sport and all robots. Let's keep sport and this world going and not let robots take it over.

Craig Dewar
Age 11

Illustration by
Melissa Afenu
Age 8

Illustration by
Daniel Ostanek
Age 8

People will run around naked just for fun and people will be able to order take-away McDonald's from their home (what luxury).

People will buy cinemas to keep in their houses and we will treasure strands of hair for the rest of our lives.

All the planets will join together to make a walkway into space so you don't need telescopes to see the stars.

Every dog will have its own personal trainer so it does not get muddled switching from one trainer to the next.

Philippa Jeffcock
Age 9

Ball

Holidays on the Moon

Shopping

The streets will have more shops.
People will be shopping,
never stopping,
just shopping, shopping,
shopping.

Declan Brook
Age 8

Illustration by
Helen Douglas
Age 10

There will be robot helpers that do the housework and all
the shopping, so that children never again have to stand in
Marks and Spencer's on a Saturday waiting for their mums.

Charlotte Goodall
Age 7

Ball

Holidays on the Moon

Illustration by
Sara Mallas
Age 9

What will we do for fun?

We might go to the park. And go on a very
long slide. There might be swings that are
very fast. We might go on an adventure
playground. We might play football. We might
go on a waterslide that has fountains that
spray you when you go past.

William Hockin
Age 5

248

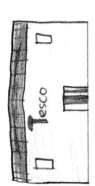

Life on mars

Millennium Homes

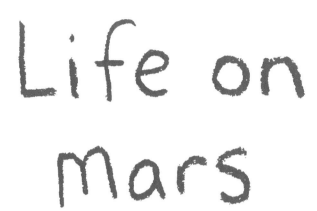

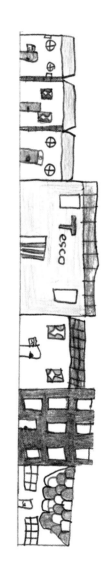

*Border illustrations by
Eleanor Pattison
Age 9*

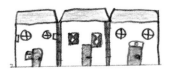

My house will be like this. I have got a living room, and I have got a bed. I like the bed. You don't get too cold or too hot in there. It has got some diamonds on the covers.

Writing and Illustration by
Annaliese Abrahams
Age 5

It will be 2000 years since Jesus was born. Jesus didn't have a proper bath in his house. His clothes were made of wool or animal skin. He did not have a car but rode on a donkey. He didn't have to go to school, he worked for his daddy. He had no television or computers to play with.

There were no hospitals. If you were poorly, you just died. Not many people could read and books were like one long loo roll.

I'm glad I live in the second millennium!

Romilly Whiteley
Age 6

Beds will be leaves and blossom woven together with stems. The main colours will be red, green, yellow and brown. It will be like a flood of colours taking over the universe. The sun would be the colours of a parrot. Your house has to be multicoloured, otherwise you get prosecuted.

Rachel Jamieson
Age 9

Illustration by
Katie McCracken
Age 5

Illustration by Victoria Hogg, Age 8

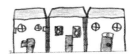 

The Knife-and-Fork-and-Spoon Robot

My robot loves to set the table. It is very useful because mummy doesn't have to ask me to set the table! The robot has knives, forks and spoons being made in his tummy. After he has set the table, some hands come out and put the bowls and plates out.

Writing and Illustration by
Lydia Labram
Age 7

The Everything Robot
Washes up for you.
Even plays football.

When you get up in the morning a hairbrush comes and brushes your hair. If you don't get up out of bed in the morning the bed squashes you and folds you in a sandwich. If you still don't get up it hits you with a stick and if that doesn't work, it shakes you.

Andrew Noakley
Age 7

Writing and Illustration by
Joanna Bacon
Age 7

My House

It's in the countryside and it's camouflaged so if any robbers come along they can't see that it's a house.

There is also a tree that has burgers on and a very tasty jelly bush.

Writing and Illustration by Matthew Alder
Age 7

There will be a robot to do the housework. It will be made of metal and look like a real person. In its hand will be a duster and polish. Its arm will get longer to reach high places. Its feet will be a hoover and suck up the dust as it moves along. I will be able to control it from my chair by a remote control.

Writing and Illustration by
Leigh Carverhill
Age 10

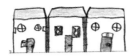 

Illustration by
Amelia Stockton
Age 4

I wonder what our houses are going to be like? Maybe they will be a castle or a fort or maybe there will be an elevator to take you up the stairs. Mum would like that.

We will have rockets to go to school in – yes! When I have homework, a smart machine could do it for me, so I'll get a gold star at school for doing it correct. Mum can put her feet up while a robot does all the washing and gardening. We will have lots of money because we have a machine. We pull the lever and the money comes out. Downstairs there is a mine full of gold. At the end of the mine, there is a seaside. We have a caravan and you can stay there.

David Robertson
Age 8

Illustration by
Hollie Newboult
Age 9

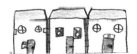 

We will have houses that will be the size of a street. They will have 21 bedrooms a thousand metres long. We will have robots to cook, wash and clean up every room in the house. We have a big safe and it's got over £60,000,000 in it.

For tea we have eggs that are hard to open and sometimes when you open them you get a little chocolate egg. But sometimes you get just an egg white or an egg yolk.

In the house we have ten thousand flowers. We have elevators to get to the rooms and floors that move. We normally have a lot of visitors. We will all have a lot of toys and sweets and really bouncy beds which will be lots of fun when friends stay.

Natalie Gray
Age 7

Illustration by Lauren Reegan
Age 8

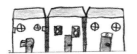 

Everyone will live in a bubble of their own. They have little arrow keys that control the bubble. We would all live under the sea and see the weirdest fish that anyone has seen! To go on holiday, a transveyor belt would take you anywhere on Earth in five minutes and ten minutes to go to space.

To go swimming you would get in an atomic mass mover and it would go anywhere underwater faster than the speed of light.

For school, the children would teach the teachers, because the teachers would not be allowed to have special brain food, but children are.

Paige Johannessen
Age 8

Illustration by Callum Mortimer
Age 9

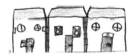 

Illustration by
Emma Dawkins
Age 6

Houses will be much smaller than they are now.
This is because there won't be much land left once all the
new houses and towns that go with them are built. We might
also run out of bricks for the walls and tiles for the roofs, so
things like thatched roofs may become popular again.

Houses will be built in places that wouldn't normally be
developed now, but because of the lack of land, fields that are
now used for growing crops and flowers will be built on.

Houses will not have big driveways and garages to try to
make people only have one car per family so that they do
not produce harmful fumes.

Gardens will also be smaller so that more houses can be
built on a piece of land and they will be built closer together.

Jessica Day
Age 8

Home Sweet Home of the Future

The moon: a deserted, ancient, dusty colossal piece of rock and dirt. Not any more! We can transform this dull planet into a regular family's dream come true.

What's on the planet?

New transport! For when you feel you want to visit grandma back on Earth, a warp-speed mini shuttle is what you need. For inside, you can hire a sort of modernized golf buggy.

There will also be a wide range of amusements for all ages, including lots of homes (of course).

The tunnels are another thing I should mention. There are four tunnels: North, South, East and West Tunnel. All four tunnels join in the middle of the moon. It's an easy way to get around the planet.

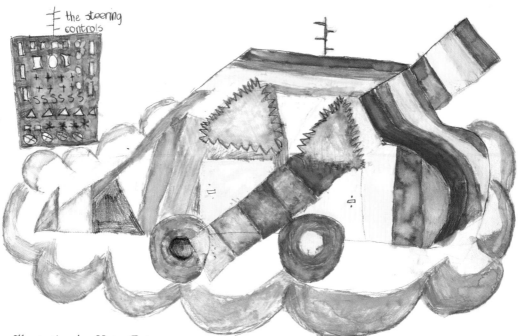

Illustration by Katy Cotgrave
Age 8

The Rainbow Machine

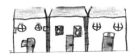

Money and Trading

Money on the moon is only used for prices such as £1,000,000 and over. Other prices under this amount are usually paid by trading, so it's very straightforward.

Katie Hodgson
Age 9

Illustration by Sarah Fitzpatrick
Age 6

One day I came to the beach and my house had moved to the sea! When I went inside, I found an octopus called Freddie. There was a shell cooker and for the table legs there were fish stuck together. There were special light bulbs made from all the creatures in the sea and there were lots of fish and crab robots to tidy up for me.

Ellie Potter
Age 7

My idea is a talking washing machine, so when you put it on and put the clothes in it will say, 'That is enough for me.' When you sit down the washing machine will sing and it will make you laugh very much. When it is finished it will say, 'I am finished, so can you come and turn me off, please?' So you have to get up and turn it off. When you turn it off it sings at you very much and it is very nice to hear.

In the morning the washing machine calls your name and you have to get up. When you have your breakfast the washing machine gets his long arm and gets the bowls out and the cereals and he puts the milk in the bowl and he puts the arm back in. When you have eaten your breakfast the washing machine washes up for you and washes everything properly.

A Washing Robot
Illustration by
Yasmeen Chouhan
Age 6

Sarah Kane
Age 9

My robot can:
paint,
hoover,
wash,
pick up.

Writing and Illustration by
Iain Gordon
Age 5

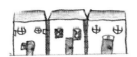 

Our houses would be underwater and we would live in tall, glass, dome-like buildings with waterslides shaped like sea monsters to scare away sharks. The reason that houses should be underwater is to keep children away from busy roads and so that, if they fall, they won't hurt themselves.

Chiara Pelizzari
Age 9

Kiss Me, I'm the Cleaner
Illustration by Pia Kingan
Age 8

In the year 2000 I think a bathroom will be made for men. This bathroom will have a fridge in it so they do not have to wait until they come out to have a beer. It will also have a 36-inch colour TV. If your wife cooks dinner, tell her to throw it in the bin. (I didn't tell you there is a cooker and lots of places for food.) We men are the best cooks in the world. No women cooks are better than us men.

Pat Kennedy
Age 11

There will be more people, so more homes will be needed. Many homes will be built in cliffs like the cavemen did, but more modern in design. Some homes will have to be built underground. The roof of the building will have grass instead of tiles. This way farmers can grow crops for food or graze cattle.

A part of each roof will be solar tiled. There may even be greenhouses in the homes to provide people with fresh fruit and vegetables.

With underground homes it means land will be available to grow enough food for everyone.

Michael Fletcher
Age 9

Millennium Home

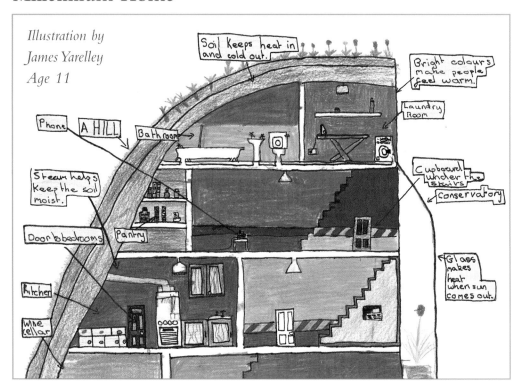

Illustration by James Yarelley Age 11

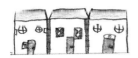 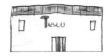

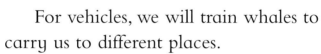

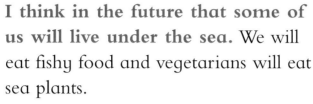

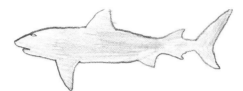

I think in the future that some of us will live under the sea. We will eat fishy food and vegetarians will eat sea plants.

For entertainment under the sea there will be diving, exploring the corals and swimming. Maybe there will be underwater shark and dolphin chariot racing and the prize would be a holiday to the surface.

For vehicles, we will train whales to carry us to different places.

Underwater there will also be different resorts. These will be museums, shopping centres, arcades and lots of science labs. They would all be made of glass so that we could see the beautiful fish. Maybe in the year 3000 we shall all have gills.

Writing and Illustrations by
Sara Williams
Age 10

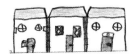 
My invention for the millennium would be a lift in a house because if you were disabled and you had to have a wheelchair, you would not be able to get up the stairs. In the lift there will be a computer that you can talk to. You could order a cup of tea on the computer if you got stuck in the lift, while you waited for help.

Writing and Illustration by
Katie Hurst
Age 9

Everything can talk in the thing I invented. The house can talk, the windows can talk, the tree can talk and the fish can talk.

Writing and Illustration by
Julia Purves
Age 6

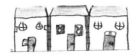 

Mr Clean is the world's best cleaning machine. As he moves he has a little hoover-type pipe that sucks up dust. To protect the ozone layer he runs on the dust that he hoovers up. As protection against robbers he has lasers in his eyes.

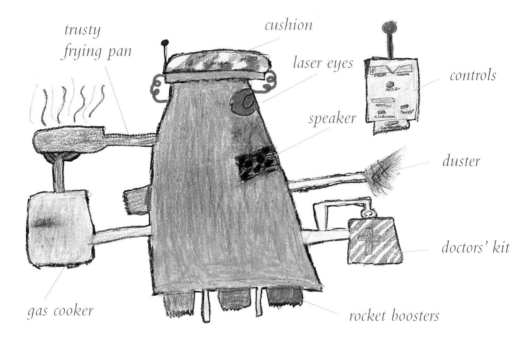

trusty
frying pan

cushion

laser eyes

controls

speaker

duster

doctors' kit

gas cooker

rocket boosters

No need for a doctor with Mr Clean – he has a never-ending supply of plasters, bandages and medicine tablets.

House-cleaning maids are a bit old-fashioned. So Mr Clean's one-swipe dusters will keep the wall clean for two weeks.

He gets around by three rocket boosters and one at the back so he doesn't go zooming into space. He has a dust-run cooker and a recycled metal frying pan.

Just in case your feet are sore after a hard day's work, Mr Clean comes to the rescue with his ultra-soft cushion. All you have to do is press the controls.

Writing and Illustration by
Don Drummond
Age 9

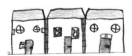 

Illustration by Kirsty Ward
Age 9

Houses will have lots of different jobs for robots, so you can lie on your bed eating chocolate all the time and you don't need to worry about brushing your teeth because the robot will do it for you. In the future I think beds will have little secret pockets in them. You can put chocolate in there without your mum and dad knowing. The bed could turn over, then turn back. You would see the real bedclothes and you wouldn't have to make the bed.

If you went down the stairs and asked your mum for a toy and she said no, there could be a goody box so you could get your toy.

Matthew Earnshaw
Age 7

A Helpful Robot
Illustration by
Lewis McCloy
Age 5

Inside my house it is very warm. You press a button and the bed flings down the TV and the chair floats.

I have a robot spider that cleans up the webs in the attic. The brush is tied to a spring. It bounces up and down. While it is bouncing up and down it cleans the house.

Jacob Stimson
Age 6

This garden is for the future because the turf is in boxes and the water is below it. The summer house is normal. The flowers must grow well in water, too, because it is two feet deep. The liner is double thick. Further back there are more turf boxes. This is for pleasure and peace. You could come here to relax and calm down. Life will go on.

Writing and Illustration by
Theo Gordon
Age 8

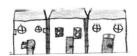 

I think our houses will look like famous people.
I would like my house to look like Brad Pitt. In our houses we will have man-size TVs and couches from the floor to the ceiling. In the bedrooms a girl will have a pink room with fluffy pillows and fluffy blankets and see-through curtains around her bed.

In a boy's room he will have a blue wall and scattered toys all over the room and it will be so dirty that his robot will have to clean it up every week. In the kitchen you'll have a robot to do all the cooking and cleaning for you.

Sarah Concar
Age 9

The Wobbly Food Home

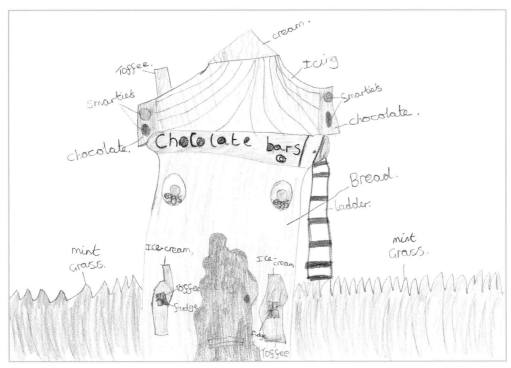

Illustration by Stephanie Cheney
Age 9

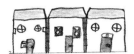 

I would like every house to be a mansion especially the houses around Southport and Windrows. I would like swimming pools to be made in every back yard, too.

Rebecca Mount
Age 10

Illustration by Steven Sparks
Age 9

My house will be on stilts in case there is a flood of water. In the new millennium my home will be able to fly. My home will be gold and silver with gold plants and silver bushes. It's going to be the best home in the whole wide world. The windows will have locks on to stop robbers coming in.

Rebecca Wyatt
Age 6

An Argumentative Planet

War and Peace

Border illustrations by
Andrew Goode
Age 9

In the future these weapons will be useful:
- The magic sword is used because when you spin round with the sword, it spins out rays.
- The giant's knife is the same as the magic sword.
- The best shield is the mirror shield because it reflects magical powers.
- The lance of truth lets you see through walls.
- The bombchu is a bomb that moves.
- The arrows are all good, but the best is the light arrow.
- The Gaullites lift up heavy things like boulders.

Imran Basri
Age 7

I think the new millennium will be excellent because I think smoking and drugs should be banned because they get people arrested and put into jail for the rest of their lives.

I am not looking forward to the new millennium because I am frightened of the war because the bombs might hit Scunthorpe.

Carra Dixon
Age 8

Illustration by
Anthony Judd
Age 8

Illustration by
Jamie Roberts
Age 6

It was the fourth of April 2099, and I was sitting in my flat saying, 'Yes! I'll stay alive for ever, yes!' These flats have a special power that keeps you alive for ever. I could not go out because of the pollution. Then I thought, 'Ah, my robot! He will go out for me.' So I typed in the shopping command and my robot went shopping for my food.

A few days later, the monsters from Venus came to town. I saw them on my computer screen. The spaceship looked green and brown, but as it got closer it was actually white. The monsters started to sit on my little car. These cars tried to clean the air as well as move along.

Fortunately there were no children out because there was no school. The teacher gave lessons through video phones. The monsters were highly dangerous. We gave the order, 'Shoot the exploder bombs,' but they failed. We tried a Hades bomb and it blew them up. Hooray!

Christopher Malton
Age 7

Monsters from Mercury

Monsters from Mercury have taken over our planet.

In the year 2500 they arrived in silver, silent spaceships.

Lanky, loud, slimy green tentacles, eyes bulging, flashing like
  light bulbs.

Lost and lonely, scared and searching, we travelled the planet
  in search of a solution.

Elastic creatures killing and maiming, trying to take over our
  world,

Neptune, our saviour, we travelled for weeks silently slipping
  through space.

Nearer and nearer, our hopes higher and higher,

In space we floated, hopeful but frightened, our home, Earth,
  a distant dream.

Uranus, Saturn and Jupiter we passed on our journey,

Monsters from Mercury have taken over our planet.

Niall Scothern
Age 8

Illustration by
Bethany Ballantyne
Age 5

Illustration by
Laura Stephen
Age 9

In the year 2000 I'd like to see peace. If there was peace, there would be no guns, no wars and especially no murdering. They would be banned. There would be no need for police.

But there are other wishes I'd like to make, like having no gravity. We would have to tie ourselves to the chairs and beds. Everything would have to be tied down. We would float around like crazy. Our houses would float, too.

I'd like a funfair in every back garden. It would be cool. My brother would love the bumper cars.

One other wish I'd like to make is that no more animals are hunted. I love animals, you see, and I keep wondering which one will become extinct next.

Molly Aylesbury
Age 9

Kosovo in the Millennium

Wandering beggars roaming the streets,
Bombed buildings everywhere.
The only faces to see are sad and dirty.
Mothers with crying babies in their arms,
And toddlers walking slowly behind.
They are so grateful for even a penny.

Wounded young men, lying on the streets,
Crying out in pain.
They are so thin from lack of food,
No pillows and no support.
Nothing can comfort them after what they've been through.
Family and friends far away.

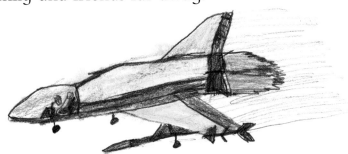

Georgina Cooper
Age 11

Illustration by
Matthew Mayor
Age 8

In the year 2099 I personally think Robocop 2000 will take over the world. Mad scientists control him from the air. He has features like knife, revolver, rocket watch, bullet-proof vest and firepower. He will then try to conquer the universe. The millennium bug will not affect his radio control and his microchip has special moves like helicopter kick and triple punch.

Thomas Pugh
Age 8

I hope in the next millennium there won't be any more wars so that adults and children will be happy again.

My invention for stopping wars will be a little box, so you can carry it around with you. If there is a war you just press 'W' and the war will stop. It will be made out of plastic, so it won't break.

Everyone in the whole wide world will have one. As well as being used to stop wars like the one in Kosovo, it can be used to stop people falling out.

I think it will be a good invention because there is nothing like it, and it would mean that everyone will be happy because there is peace.

Mollie Occomore
Age 7

War will be different. I think soldiers will wear different armour. They might even have peculiar weapons. They might fire vegetables like carrots, cauliflower, sprouts, cabbage, tomatoes, potatoes, cucumber and chicken.

Nicholas Forbes
Age 7

Policeman in the new millennium

Illustration by
Matthew Mayor
Age 8

As we are moving into a new millennium, I really think that this should be a new chance for world peace. There should be no more wars, because lots of people are killed when they haven't even done anything wrong. I think that all countries should sign a contract that means they can never fight again.

Many countries invade other countries because they just want to rule them. They should be happy with what they have. I think that the world should have one language, one currency and one religion, because sometimes countries have wars over these kinds of things and this would stop that happening.

Andrew Goode
Age 9

Illustration by
Rhodri Manning
Age 9

Illustration by
Georgina Tate
Age 7

My thought is that millions of people are getting all excited because it's 2000 years A.D.

I hardly expect countries will stop having wars and fighting each other.

Land mines won't stop killing and harming people.

Life will still be hard for millions of people all around the globe.

Everyone won't stop suffering or dying from illnesses.

Nothing is going to make any real difference.

Natural disasters like forest fires, storms, hurricanes and floods will still happen.

It won't stop burglars and thugs from robbing and harming homes and people.

Unless we change our ways . . .

Millennium – nothing will really change.

Richard Sullivan
Age 9

After a nuclear war against Iraq, Britain has been turned into rubble. The remains of the population fight each other to their deaths in giant mechs. They fight in a giant arena made up of what used to be London. Six mechs fight at once, but only one mech comes out. To make it harder, they have placed missile launchers and machine gun turrets around the battleground.

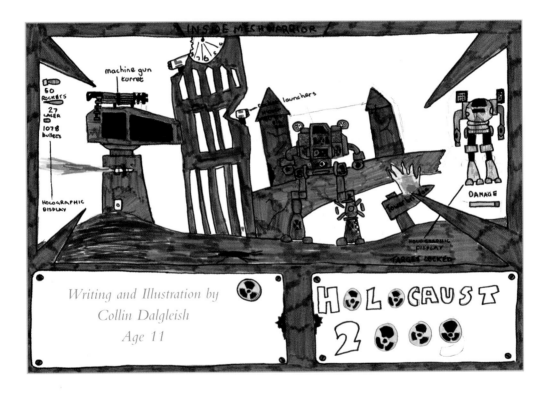

Writing and Illustration by Collin Dalgleish Age 11

I wish that there could be no war and just peace, because when I see all those refugees on the television, I always think that if I was in that condition I would not like it at all. I hope that all the homeless people on the streets will become like us. We should all be the same.

Jody Falla
Age 9

Across the Black Sky

Blinding heat splits the air,
The droning of engines fills the world with sound.
The shatter and cracking retort of the shells
Is all around, and the fiery red explosions flame
Across the black sky.

Then a great flash of luminous light blinds the world,
And a huge mushroom cloud bursts into the
Atmosphere and all the rumblings have ceased.
And the world is split open,
Wide open,
And down the crevice the bowels of the Earth lie
Glistening in their own blood.

The war-torn Earth is in torment
As the nuclear holocaust descends,
And a veil of white dust covers the heavens.
For many and for all it would be the last glimpse
They had . . .

Connor Donahue
Age 11

Illustrated by
Craig Scott
Age 7

I think kids will rule the universe. Instead of adults teaching children, children will teach adults how to be a kid, e.g. not tidying your room, not eating your dinner and only eating sweets and chocolate.

There will be one most powerful country, and it's Ireland. Ireland rules the universe. Ireland first takes over America, then the world, then the moon, then the universe. You see, Ireland's men, women and children were all very clever and they made a type of chocolate that made people worship Ireland.

After Ireland took over the world, it started on the other planets like the moon and Mars, and now, because of the clever people of Ireland, we can live on other planets.

I know you don't believe me, but when kids take over the world, anything can happen.

Róisín O'Reilly
Age 10

Illustration by Siobhan Hearns
Age 12

An Argumentative Planet

When I grow up I wish Star Wars was real and all the good guys were invisible and the bad guys weren't invisible. All the good guys would win and the bad guys would lose.

Jamel Burke
Age 6

Star Wars
Illustration by
Khadija Bouncir
Age 7

Will our future be a blast, or a repeating image of our past? I mean, look at *Space 1999*, a TV programme from the '60s. Have we established a way of living on the moon? Do we carry laser guns? When comes the time we can live in everlasting peace?

No, no, never! It may be human nature to discover, but will it only end when we have collected all power over the universe? And as we know that will never happen, will we be destroyed by our thirst for knowledge and power?

John Norton
Age 9

Illustration by
Matthew Biggs
Age 7

The millennium will bring doom to all mankind. First earthquakes will tear apart most major cities, as the result of an experiment involving a rabbit and a crate of bananas.

These earthquakes are so violent they create a lava flow to many dead volcanoes, causing them to erupt. The eruptions are explosive, and the huge flows of rock and ash will wipe out the rest of America. The explosions as power plants are destroyed send a signal to aliens from a distant galaxy, who just happen to be passing by, and trigger an attack.

The aliens come down in their thousands, and beam up whole buildings with their high-tech spaceships. Soon most remaining cities are gone and, knowing the earthlings are defenceless, the aliens land and seize power over the Earth.

Britain is conquered by them, and all humans who live there are sent to Pluto, where they freeze to death. They keep Tony Blair, and make him their slave.

Gradually the aliens take over the world, leaving only Tony Blair and two goldfish as original inhabitants of the Earth, which will be populated by billions of creatures from a far-off world.

Aimee Lockwood
Age 11

Today there are many wars and, if wars were stopped, countries would save thousands of pounds. As a result, there wouldn't be many people starving in countries like Brazil, Africa and Indonesia.

Rebecca Mount
Age 10

Another Millennium

Is the millennium
Just another date?
Or the last phase
In this planet's fate?

Forgotten trees,
Never seen,
And animal life
A mythical dream.

An argumentative planet,
Globally warm.
A place of sadness
Where disease can swarm.

A giant rush,
The human race,
Stumbling onward
To oblivious space.

Our planet laid waste,
Sucked dry like a prune.
Hurtling through space,
As dead as our moon.

Is the millennium
Just another date?
Or a chance to change
Before it's too late?

Mhairi Murdoch
Age 11

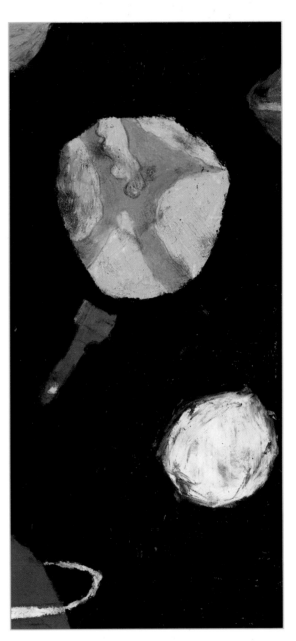

Illustration by
Harriet McDaniel
Age 9

An Argumentative Planet

In 2000 there will be no government.
We will have two queens.

James Keating
Age 6

I think that wars will go on, because we have never been civilized people. And we will not have to go to school, because everybody will have a computer to work on. Pluto will be the best holiday resort in the universe, with a lot of rooms and beaches. We will live on Saturn when wars are on. We will drive flying cars in the moonlight and make alien friends.

Charlotte Bennett
Age 10

Illustration by
Craig Scott
Age 7

Punishment for doing crimes might be death, or it might be cleaning bathrooms for 20 years and you won't get paid.

Joshua Jones
Age 11

I hope that the year 2000 will bring happiness to a lot of poor families. I hope that they have clothes and shoes to run about and play in. Their homes should be quite big and should not have any leaks.

Millions of children die every day because they are neglected and catch many illnesses due to poor nutrition. Children should receive medical help from nurses and doctors from all over the world. Children should not be allowed on the streets to beg for food.

I really hope that everyone, especially the children, in our country and in all the better-off countries in the world, will help these people who are in very desperate need.

Let's make the year 2000 a caring year.

Claire Rankin
Age 10

Illustration by Rebecca Tidey
Age 5

Save the World

The world is in such an awful state,
When I'm older I'll make it great.
No more wars or pollution.
How I wish I could find a solution.
No more oil in the sea.
But this won't happen just because of me.
So I'll find some people to help me,
And together we'll save the
WORLD!

Writing and Illustration by
Tamsin Elliott
Age 8

In the millennium black and white will unite and live as one

Illustration by
Louise Williams
Age 11

I have been thinking about what our world would be like if there was no racism.

I was watching the news about Stephen Lawrence. He was murdered by a group of young teenagers in a racist attack. He was not doing any harm to any of the boys that night. I asked myself how and why this happened.

I thought about my friends. I am black and I have black friends and white friends. We are all the same. We play the same games, we eat the same type of food and we wear the same style of clothes. The only difference is the colour of our skin. We are all children . . . we are all human beings.

My hope is that in the new millennium people will learn to live together, no matter what colour they are. Everybody is special, and if we all learn to love and respect each other, our world will be a special place.

Dominique Carter
Age 9

Mum Drives a Rocket Blaster

Life in the Future

Border illustrations by
Susan Millar
Age 7

 **There will be escalators instead of stairs** and you just have to press a red button to get a large roast dinner with a second course. Instead of cars, small orange vehicles can always be seen in the sky. They have four seats, and a blackcurrant drinking fountain. Everything will be made out of jelly. Gradually the Earth will become square. A jumbo tree can be seen and it grows chewing gum.

Noodles will be a popular food, and there will be a café where people come to try out different sorts. People will have larger brains, so they can multiply high numbers in a matter of seconds. People's houses are small and round, and there are twenty rooms on each floor. Bouncy castles do not exist, because everything is already made from jelly. Fashion is another thing. People like to wear long black bin-liners and everyone has pink hair.

Writing and Illustrations by
Gilly Seymour
Age 8

NEWS 2000

New Year celebrations end in the dark!
Big new year party in London ends in disaster when lights go out. Thousands of people stranded in city centre.

Illustration by Holly Short
Age 5

Genetically modified apples, which resist all known diseases and are bigger and more tasty, have been found to turn people green.

Mr Willy Wonka invents new chewing gum for dinner. We interviewed Mr Wonka and this is what he said: 'I'm very proud of it. It's fantastic.'

Planes land at midnight. Old-style planes were forced to land when computers failed. Hundreds of people were left in foreign countries.
New space vehicles are being sent to the rescue.

Illustration by Liam Gowing
Age 4

Dentists have invented a paint which can be painted onto teeth. This means teeth will never go bad. You can eat as many sweets as you like.

Hannah Bowditch
Age 8

We go to the moon for a holiday in our own spaceships. We go space-jet skiing and have a feast of cheese, because it really is made of it! It takes three seconds to go to Dublin instead of three hours, because we have transporters which you walk into and say where you want to go.

Our clothes are silver and gold and never get dirty. Food is just a tablet which tastes of chocolate but is good for you. Water tastes of Coke, but doesn't rot your teeth! YIPPEE!

Children's games are 'Spacemen and Aliens', 'Starcops and Martians' and 'Space Station Zebra'. Starcops have protection lasers and they know children's ages just by putting their hands into a lunar metal box. Any baddies are sent to the fourth dimension until their teeth fall out.

S'LONG . . . ZZZZZZAPPPPP!!!!

Stephen McKelvie
Age 8

Illustration by
Laura Northover
Age 7

Our houses will look the same on the outside but the house's roof will have little eyes in it. They will watch for trouble, and when there is trouble the house will have two legs to run away with.

There will be different new inventions for different people. There will be:

- a third arm for mothers who want one
- a talking science lab for scientists
- a submarine in the shape of a crocodile so that people could look underwater in a swamp

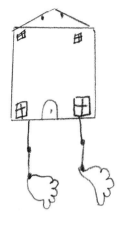

For entertainment we will go and watch things like cactus fighting, which has two men hitting each other with cacti.

Writing and Illustration by
Emily Reece
Age 9

a third arm for mothers

1472 Flying House
Flower Dry Road
Ceath
Pladly
UK
Earth

Dear Mum,

The world is such a terrible place, even though we are ruled by genetically modified people. Some countries with genetically modified people have been fixed with computer chips that control them. The creator is half human, half robot. His name is Dr Fran.

I'm one of the only human humans around here. I'm considered dumb. I am writing to you from a flying house. I know it sounds great, but cameras are everywhere.

Don't come back!

Yours sincerely,

Holly

*Holly Bryant
Age 9*

*Illustrations by
Ellie Hair
Age 6*

New inventions might give us unlimited cheap energy that does not pollute the atmosphere. By using mirrors in space, it might be possible to have 24 hours of daylight all over the Earth. This would be an advantage in winter. It might even be that we do not need to sleep!

We will have new medicines to help us fight diseases. Scientists might even be able to find cures for major killers like heart disease and cancer.

Houses will be constructed from new materials which will be more environmentally friendly, and you will be able to control doors, curtains, lights, televisions and cookers by voice command.

New foods will be invented, which will be resistant to disease and insects, and will grow where it is presently very difficult to grow crops, i.e. certain parts of Africa and deserts. This will help to solve the world's hunger problems.

Liam Robinson
Age 9

Illustration by
Jessica Rae
Age 12

The Year Three Thousand

It is the year three thousand,
And things are different now.
And in this little poem,
I'm going to tell you how.

We don't have electricity,
Or gas or oil for power.
We generate it from the sun,
Through a tall thin tower.

Cities are mainly underground,
With parks and pools on top.
We jump in a space train bubble,
And zap from shop to shop.

They work us very hard at school,
But then our time's our own.
I play with my personal robot
And gremlin when I get home.

Computers are in every room,
We hardly move around.
They do every bit of work
As soon as we give the sound.

Illustrations by
Georgia Sim
Age 7

We are on the 'Outernet',
I have a friend on Mars.
His skin is green and wrinkly,
And he looks like a flower vase.

We are saving for our holiday
To Jupiter this year.
We will be shot there in a capsule
And arrive this time last year.

Illustration by Georgia Sim
Age 7

Joel Rees
Age 9

We will have:
- Everlasting toothpaste
- Indestructible trousers
- Flying skateboards
- Robots that do all our work
- Unpuncturable footballs

What will happen:
- Teachers will give us fizzy drinks
- Dinosaurs will inhabit the Earth
- We'll all have a personal jet
- Rollerblades will have 64 gears
- Toilets will have auto-flush
- Seas will be cleaner than now
- Teachers will teach us easy work

Writing and Illustration by
Matthew Collinge
Age 9

Fun and Games

We will wake up every morning,
And a button will be pressed.
Then we will fall through a trapdoor,
And be in the kitchen fully dressed.
Your breakfast will come running –
Rainbow Squares in a milky pool.
You eat it very quickly,
Then go to boring school.
You go zooming through the air,
With a rocket on your back.
You go flying through the classroom,
And sit down with a clack.
No boring Maths, just fun and games,
Like catapulting teachers.
They fly to the next planet
Like a mass of funny creatures!
After school you fly back home,
Soaring like a plane.
You eat your tea then go to bed,
Then the whole day starts again.

Chloe Hibbert
Age 10

Illustration by
Thomas Nix
Age 7

Hi! My name's Lackzoo.
I live in the year 2050.

    My life's really interesting. My mum drives a rocket blaster to work. Her work's great. It's talking to aliens to solve their problems, so I meet loads of interesting people.

me

    I've got a little box that turns me into a fly and I go around spying on people. My house is made of steel and it's a triangular shape. I've got my own robot, so I don't need a friend. He's called Falamph.

    My dad's got a hat and when you put it on you go back in time. He won't let me use it, but yesterday I went to his room and went back in time to give you this letter.

Writing and Illustrations by
Ellen Roberts
Age 9

Illustration by
Amy Hughes
Age 9

My personal communicating TV hangs upon the wall,
Informing me that a computerised concert is at the Albert Hall.
Looking through my heat-conserving windows,
Longing to join my friends at the cyber-fashion shows,
Everyone is wearing the latest superventilated clothes!
Next I change into my air-conditioned dress –
Not for us hot, sticky, tired and distressed.
In this millennium, technology is the game.
Under new rules, not for long will things stay the same.
Millennium is fun! How great it is to be in the 21st century!

Lizzie Rowe
Age 10

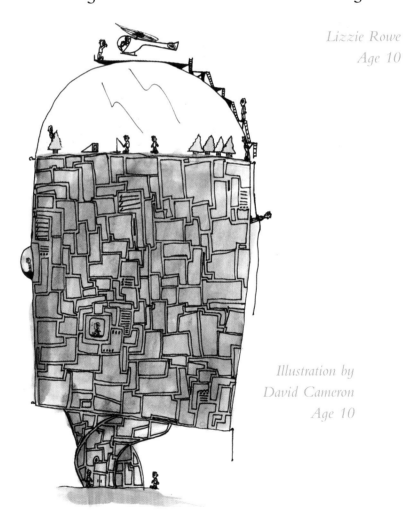

Illustration by
David Cameron
Age 10

History Lesson

I am living in the year 2532. We are learning about the later Elizabethans. We have been looking at a computer of their time. It is very primitive and the games are awful. They must have got really bored.

We learnt about a place called a 'safari park' for endangered animals. If you ask me, poachers would have got in, no trouble. Now the endangered animals have been moved up to the moon and security is high, so poachers cannot go there, and the gravity is just right, so the animals don't float around. They are all kept in domes with different environments – jungle, forest, flatland, pasture – so the animals will always be safe.

The other day we were looking at 20th century human skulls. We noticed that ours are bigger. That means we must have bigger brains. No wonder they were so stupid!

Iain Pattison
Age 10

computers

Illustration by
Laura Dolan
Age 5

Illustration by Hannah Mumford
Age 8

Lots of New Things

The millennium will bring lots of new things,
Especially Wills, our handsome new king.
You can choose a new face
Or have a house in space.
They've invented a dog chew to make dogs talk,
And a magic new lead to take them for walks.
The man next door has bought a house on Mars,
And now you can even buy flying cars.
A magic pill for your grandma
Will make her look like a superstar.
Now all my friends are going to the Millennium Dome
But I'm quite happy to stay at home.

Becky Campbell
Age 10

Life in the millennium will be so much fun.
We will fly to school on jet-packs, powered by the sun.
We will travel anywhere we like on a solar-heated train,
And even to the moon on a super jet aeroplane.
The robots in our houses will do anything we wish.
Our mums' lives will be easier, they won't have to clean a dish.
We won't have to do any shopping, we can do it very quick,
By sitting at the computer and giving the mouse a click.
You order off the Internet and they deliver it to your door.
You can pay them with your credit card
Or send a cheque to the store.
You will feel safe at all times, there won't be gangs or riots,
Robocops will patrol the streets to keep them safe and quiet.
When you phone your friends you will see their faces too,
So you'd better watch out if someone phones you and you're
    sitting on the loo.
The sweeties will be bigger, our teeth will not decay,
Because the dentist made an invention to keep the plaque away.
Life in the millennium is going to be great.
Hurray! Only a few more months to wait!

John-Duncan Campbell
Age 10

Illustration by David Whyte
Age 8

Illustration by Jennifer Molloy
Age 10

1st January 2000

Bleep, bleep – 'Good morning, Jeff. Please go to the bathroom. Your shower is running.' I stepped into the shower, the door shut behind me, and gentle hands shampooed my hair. The water turned off automatically and blow-driers dried my whole body. My toothbrush, an electronic one, left my mouth sparkling. My bed was made when I returned and my clothes for the day were laid on the bed, having first been checked that they were suitable for the day's weather.

I quickly swallowed my breakfast in capsule form. I was going to meet some friends for a game of cyber rugby in the arcade. I travelled by a solar-powered hoverboard which automatically adjusted to the correct speed limits and traffic

light commands. I was scanned into the arcade and credit loaded onto my card.

After an enjoyable afternoon, I returned home. My daily nutritional capsule was left for me and I caught up on my e-mail. Soothing music and low lights suggested bedtime. I yawned, put on my pyjamas and snuggled into my sleeping chamber, where I soundly slept the recommended time for my age.

Jeff Bailey
Age 12

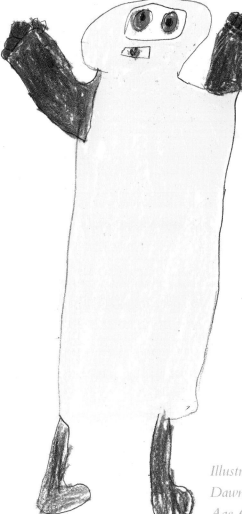

We might invent some things called plastic glasses that keep the wind out of our eyes, so we can see where we are going when it is really, really windy. Nobody else could see the plastic glasses, so you could go out to a marvellous restaurant and no one would notice, because plastic is see-through.

Alice Lamb
Age 7

Illustration by
Dawn Whitworth
Age 6

Illustration by
Adrienne Golding
Age 11

Hello, I'm Lucy. I'm 63 years old. I'm glad I've lived into the next century – a whole new era.

My house is wonderful and extremely futuristic. It has silver everything, even my grass! It cost around 20,000 euros. Sorry, that's our new currency. It's good, because we don't have to change our money when we go to any European country. But now there is no Britain, just 'The Euro Countries'. We are looked on as one country. We can drive across the English Channel over a bridge. We don't have passports, but microchips in our necks.

Now every living person is cloned, and the clone is kept in the basement of the person's house. If you have any trouble with your organs, there is an exact donor. But in 2023 there

was a great scandal. Millions (slight exaggeration) of clones escaped. They had to be shot, which caused great controversy.

In case you're wondering, I did have a husband. Well, I still do, kind of. You see, he was part of an experiment to freeze people while they are alive, so that they can be brought back to life. Seven people were frozen and said to be brought back to life in 2071.

Three of my children are on holiday on Mars and my other son lives on Pluto. They haven't got the gadgets we have and are still working to see if other people can survive there. He lives in a gigantic house full of oxygen. They keep having to send supplies to him.

So, there is my life. The life of the future. I suppose you could say the life of dreams, hopes and expectations.

Lucy Lyons
Age 11

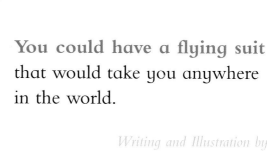

You could have a flying suit that would take you anywhere in the world.

Writing and Illustration by
Sophie Booth
Age 7

Monday 2nd April, 2098

I woke up this morning and couldn't find my lap-top computer for school. I asked all the robot maids, but they're all really dopey. I shall have to re-programme them.

The instant-button restaurant gave me all the wrong food today. I asked for porridge with golden syrup on, and it gave me a piece of stale bread. I still can't believe people one hundred years ago used to make their own food!

School was off today because our teacher had broken. For the rest of the day I just played with my new virtual reality, supersonic helmet and got the maids to fix the instant-button restaurant.

I really enjoy having computers and robots to do things for me, but I wouldn't mind a real friend for a change.

Writing and Illustration by
Hannah Bagnall
Age 11

My Diary in the Year 2000

15th Jan.

Guess what? Virtual school was actually fun. In History we learnt that people in the old days watched a box with tiny people inside, called a television, for entertainment! And in Geography we learnt that people used to think the Earth was round!

After school I had a quick game of computer-ball with a strange creature called a dog. Then I had to board a rocket to go to Mars as part of my Spacework. When I arrived home, I went to electro-bed.

That night I thought about school. Weren't human beings strange? I'm sure glad I'm not one.

Writing and Illustration by
Natalie Holmes
Age 11

New Brain Wash System

7.00pm	Try out new brain-wash system.
7.30pm	Find someone stupid enough to try brain-wash system.
8.30pm	Fix pay-as-you-type computer.
9.00pm	Go and see alien friend on Mars.
9.30pm	Read new computerised book.
10.00pm	Go and see new robot queen.
10.30pm	Play on Nintendo 74.
11.00pm	So tired, go to Tell-Tell-Story Bed.
7.00am	Get out of Tell-Tell-Story Bed.
7.30am	Play cards with my robot.
8.00am	Go to school.
8.15am	Go to first lesson and wait while a teacher puts a chip in my brain.
9.00am	Go home.
9.15am	Throw chip away.
9.17am	Watch TV with highly flammable robot.

Joshua Light
Age 10

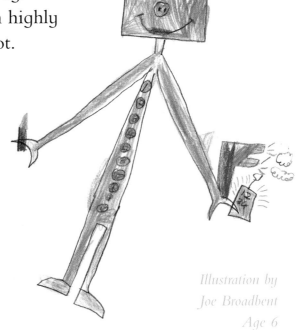

Illustration by
Joe Broadbent
Age 6

Index

Index of Contributors

Index

Index

List of Schools

Index